Congratulations.
    Your record of accomplishments
defines you as a person and as
a leader.

                    Best of Luck,
                    Bob Mulcahy

AN ATHLETIC DIRECTOR'S STORY AND THE FUTURE OF COLLEGE SPORTS IN AMERICA

AN ATHLETIC DIRECTOR'S STORY AND THE FUTURE OF COLLEGE SPORTS IN AMERICA

ROBERT E. MULCAHY III
WITH ROBERT STEWART

RUTGERS UNIVERSITY PRESS
NEW BRUNSWICK, CAMDEN, AND NEWARK,
NEW JERSEY, AND LONDON

Library of Congress Cataloging-in-Publication Data

Names: Mulcahy, Robert E., author. | Stewart, Robert, 1949– author.
Title: An athletic director's story and the future of college sports in America / by Robert
   Mulcahy III ; with Robert Stewart.
Description: [New Brunswick, NJ] : Rutgers University Press, [2020] | Includes biblio-
   graphical references and index.
Identifiers: LCCN 2019015440 | ISBN 9781978802124 (hardcover) | ISBN
   9781978802155 (mobi) | ISBN 9781978802162 (pdf) | ISBN 9781978802148 (epub)
Subjects: LCSH: Mulcahy, Robert E. | Rutgers University—Sports—History. | Athletic
   directors—New Jersey—Biography. | College sports—United States.
Classification: LCC GV697.M74 A3 2020 | DDC 796.092 [B]—dc23
LC record available at https://lccn.loc.gov/2019015440

A British Cataloging-in-Publication record for this book is available from the British
Library.

♾ The paper used in this publication meets the requirements of the American National
Standard for Information Sciences—Permanence of Paper for Printed Library Materials, ANSI Z39.48-1992.

www.rutgersuniversitypress.org

Manufactured in the United States of America

To my beloved wife, Terry—without your love, strength, and encouragement, this story would not be possible.
You have always been the wind beneath my wings.

To my children and grandchildren—you have had the unusual opportunity to experience many of the stories and events written about here from the front row. My hope is that this book serves as a lesson on how to lead a life of purpose, with faith, strength, and respect for others as your guiding principles.

CONTENTS

FOREWORD

The nation doesn't simply need what we have. It needs what we are.
—St. Teresa Benedicta

So what in God's name is this about? A question asked rhetorically countless times a day but one that is perhaps appropriate for a book by Bob
Mulcahy.

The chapters ahead address the challenges that marked his years as the
athletic director at Rutgers, with some look backs to people and events
that molded Bob. But to truly know Bob Mulcahy is to experience a lesson
in not just the *what* (What am I going to do for a career? What do I do to
handle a crisis or negotiate a deal?) but also the *how* (How can I conduct
myself with honor and integrity when the pressure is the greatest?). To
bring the same set of values when the spotlight is shining or in the quiet of
the night when no one seems to be paying attention is a lesson not lost on
those who have been at Bob's side.

If you do an internet search for business and life leadership how-to
books, a million titles come up. People are searching for guidance. As the
years go by, the content of one's character is much more telling than the job
titles on his or her curriculum vitae. People who can lead and succeed with
integrity are worth learning from. Now more than ever, when the immedi-
acy of the smartphone and its apps encourage a "ready, aim, fire" approach
to life, such models of integrity are crucial.

Prelude to a Public Service Career

When Bob was a child, his mother, Viola, loved to read him stories about great composers and political leaders who overcame shortcomings and handicaps to bring their gifts to full flower and exemplify the virtues of public service and integrity.

Mozart and Beethoven were her two favorite composers. One certainly wouldn't say these lessons from Mom gave the young man perfect pitch or even the ability to carry a tune. But the foundation for his approach to life was being laid.

Those leaders Viola educated young Bob about included the founder of the country, George Washington, and its savior, Abraham Lincoln.

At his beloved Villanova, Bob would learn from losing an election and rebound to win class president the following year. He became a sports editor and then the editor-in-chief of his college newspaper, the *Villanovan*—a truly ironic feat for someone who would spend much of the next 50 years under a high degree of media scrutiny. He was cited in *Who's Who in American Colleges* and subsequently as an Outstanding Young Man in America.

The call to service was ingrained as well as Bob joined the naval ROTC program.

Service to one's country was not questioned in those days, and his years as a naval officer on the USS *Leyte CVS-32* and USS *Tarawa CVS-40* (both sister ships to the *Intrepid*) helped foster the commitment and discipline he would need in later endeavors. Of course, he also got a dose of humility when his first turn at the helm might have been disastrous. Luckily, the captain suggested he countermand the order on the degree and speed of the maneuver, preventing the planes on the flight deck from sliding into the ocean.

During this time, Bob was counseled by one of the great influences in his life (and the life of many other prominent Catholics of the time), the Benedictine abbot Martin Burne, who served as a naval chaplain attached to the Third Marine Division and participated in the bloody invasions of Guadalcanal, Bougainville, and Guam. Young Bob was seriously considering the priesthood, but at the same time, his beloved Terry was waiting as a senior at the College of New Rochelle during his deployment. Abbot Burne knew Bob well and guided him toward a life of service in the world.

Bob came home from the Navy; married Terry, who would be the rock that his career would be built on; and settled into the family construction business. Seven children over the next 20 years would fill their home with love and challenges.

Shortly after his return, an Irish Catholic former naval officer would be elected president, and Bob, like many of his generation, was inspired by John F. Kennedy's national call to action.

Mendham, New Jersey, had not had a Democrat mayor since the days of the Whigs and the Copperheads. Bob was to change all that. He took Kennedy's challenge to enter the arena to heart and got himself elected first as a councilman and subsequently as the mayor.

But more than that, Bob left a legacy in Mendham by working with others to bring a senior citizen housing development to town and obtained financing from the U.S. Department of Agriculture through Senator Pete Williams.

He started and approved the Mendham Commons townhouses and a nursing home, both firsts. Managing in the municipal government, he created a master plan, stabilized taxes, built a new relationship with the police department, and improved the infrastructure. However, he learned a lesson in politics and human nature with the latter, as after successfully lobbying Trenton for a traffic light in town, he was hung in effigy by some of the old guard. As mayor, he shook up the old boys' network more than a bit by endorsing assemblywoman Ann Klein, the first viable woman candidate for governor.

On April 4, 1974, the Mendham *Observer-Tribune* editorialized on the mayor's departure: "Bob Mulcahy is an honest man. Not because it is to his advantage to appear this way, but because deep down that's the way he is. This honesty and seriousness of purpose meant that he had to do the best possible job as mayor that he could. He made himself available to all people at all times whether on the phone or in person. He was never too busy."[1] That trait has followed him to this day.

Trenton noticed Bob, and Ann Klein recruited him to become the deputy commissioner of the Department of Institutions and Agencies (which had a portfolio as broad as imaginable, ranging from human services to mental health, youth and family services, welfare, schools for the disabled, and prisons). It was his real introduction into understanding the marginalized and helpless in society and our mutual responsibility for helping them. As President Kennedy said in what was to be his final State of the Union address, "This country cannot afford to be materially rich and spiritually poor."[2]

Bob became New Jersey's first commissioner of corrections in 1976 after proficiently handling two riots at Trenton Prison.

Not long after, Bob was faced with the challenge of managing a hostage crisis when a knife-wielding assailant took a woman hostage in the sex offenders unit at Rahway.

Bob's reasoned, ethical approach in the face of the highly emotionally charged state of affairs allowed him to diffuse the situation, and both the hostage and knife-wielding hostage taker emerged unharmed. He chose reason over a seemingly justifiable shoot-to-kill option. How he went about it—with thoughtfulness and concern and an ear for all sides—dictated that the chosen strategy had the best chance for a safe solution. Sense conquered emotion.

In nominating Bob for the Rockefeller Public Service Award from the Woodrow Wilson School at Princeton, then New Jersey Chief Justice of the Supreme Court Richard J. Hughes noted in a letter to administrative director Ingrid W. Reed,

> Mr. Mulcahy's contributions to the citizens of New Jersey in this truly critical area are without peer. At a time when prisons across the

Bob answering reporters' questions after the prison attack, with acting corrections and parole director Richard A. Seidl (*right*) standing by. Trentonian Photos by Bob Harris.

country are the subject of both state and federal litigation to force improvement, he took the helm of the newly created New Jersey Department of Corrections. He guided this Department through its infancy and set the goals to which it still aspires. He has earned its praise throughout the country and made it a model in many areas. . . . Perhaps most profound among Mr. Mulcahy's contributions is the sense of morality and fairness that Mr. Mulcahy instilled throughout the corrections system.

Additionally in the nomination, New Jersey attorney general John Degnan said, "His inspirational ability was characterized in a plaque presented to him by his staff when he left Corrections. It read, 'you have taught us a great deal about the meaning of public service, for you epitomize what is best in government.'"

After Governor Brendan Byrne's reelection, Bob was the first to hold the newly created position of chief of staff. He was given a mandate to reorganize the governor's office.

A caring home, a Villanova education, and his naval experience were the building blocks, but something more profound ultimately shaped Bob's ability to enter the arena and face both victory and defeat with equanimity.

To truly consider Bob Mulcahy's life and career, one must first understand the profound role his faith has played in his life. Being of service to others is, to use a modern phrase, simply part of the Mulcahy DNA. It is not for show, not for reward, but for the awareness that one's own life would be somehow unsatisfied without it.

Bob's idea of a holiday with staff was to have them volunteer with his family at Eva's Soup Kitchen in Paterson, with which his wife, Terry, had a historically long involvement.

The priests and congregations who helped shape his young life would become the bishops and cardinals he would serve in his adult career—managing the unmanageable church's hospital system in Newark, known as Cathedral Healthcare, and bringing Pope John Paul II to Giants Stadium to touch 84,000 people. For his service work, Bob was awarded the Medal of St. Gregory by the Vatican at the request of the Bishop of Paterson.

Governor Byrne's two terms in office coincided with extreme difficulties in the national and regional economies. Interest and inflation rates were well into the double digits as unemployment rose and economic growth stalled. These national conditions resulted in revenue declines for the states. New Jersey faced a school funding crisis, and Governor Byrne knew the only solution was a graduated income tax despite its political unpopularity.

In accepting Governor Byrne's offer to be New Jersey's first chief of staff, Bob knew there could be no success without a great team. In what would become a hallmark of his decision-making, he reached out and brought in two of New Jersey's best, Harold Hodes and Stewart Pollock (later to become a justice of the New Jersey Supreme Court) to work with him. This would not be an administration led by sycophants and yes-men.

As incendiary as tax policy can be in politics, it pales in comparison to property rights issues. Years (perhaps decades) ahead of his time, Governor Byrne was aware that saving the precious natural resource of the New Jersey Pinelands—and protecting the irreplaceable aquifer that lay beneath it—was worth whatever political price had to be paid. This "saving" to many was a "taking" to others, particularly the property owners of the region.

But by 1979, the administration knew that rampant unregulated development in this sensitive region could never be undone. Bob's relationship and consensus building—with the keen effectiveness of deputy chief Harold Hodes—his steady hand, and his focus on the end goal were essential in getting this landmark legislation passed. It was no small feat overcoming the significant opposition from a powerful member of the governor's own party, Richard Coffee, then the chairman of the State Democratic Party and executive director of the general assembly and the construction interests in the state.

The late 1970s were a difficult time for the country. The Organization of the Petroleum Exporting Countries (OPEC) boycotts, gas lines at the stations, double-digit interest rates, and inflation were among the factors that would cost a president his reelection. In the Northeast, the situation was particularly bleak.

The Coalition of Northeast Governors (CONEG) was formed to present a united bipartisan front on important issues that were facing the federal government.

Governor Byrne became the chairman, and Bob succeeded Massachusetts lieutenant governor Tommy O'Neill as the chair of the advisory board of CONEG and was responsible for overseeing their legislative initiatives, including testifying before Congress. That position required balancing the goals of individual states, the philosophies of different parties, and the egos of governors to find common ground that would result in policy steps to help the region. Marilyn Thompson managed not only Governor Byrne's Washington office but also the coalition office with great skill, being in no small way responsible for much of CONEG's success. She became a lifelong friend.

Leadership requires being unafraid of listening to the counsel of strong-willed, smart colleagues and staffers. Leadership also takes consensus building. In politics and business, there are those who will see every transaction as marked with winners and losers. Bob learned and taught others that it is far more productive to give the "loser" a gracious way out, as in politics you may well need his or her vote next week, and in business you are very likely to see this person again down the road. Soon thereafter, Bob was called to become the president and CEO of the New Jersey Sports and Exposition Authority (NJSEA), which aimed to move New Jersey from the back row of professional sports, entertainment, and events to the forefront of the world stage.

Daring Leadership in the Sports Arena

In his years at the NJSEA, Bob became a board member of the National Football Foundation (NFF) and College Hall of Fame as his friend and NJSEA chairman Jon Hanson ascended to head that prestigious organization as well.

Coincidentally, at the NFF banquet in 1961, President Kennedy called to mind the words of one of his favorite presidents: "Theodore Roosevelt once said, 'The credit belongs to the man who is actually in the arena—whose face is marred by dust and sweat and blood . . . who knows the great enthusiasms, the great devotions—and spends himself in a worthy cause—who at best if he wins knows the thrills of high achievement—and if he fails at least fails while daring greatly—so that his place shall never be with those cold and timid souls who know neither victory or defeat.'"[3]

Bob believed you had to be in the arena.

After the flamboyant Sonny Werblin created the NJSEA, becoming its first chairman and CEO, and spearheaded the construction of the stadium and racetrack at the Meadowlands Sports Complex, he headed to Madison Square Garden. In short order, two of his successors came and went.

Could Bob Mulcahy stabilize the business of this still new attraction? Surely he was not flashy; he was not going to be hanging out at the 21 Club with Joe Namath.

But as Governor Byrne said in 2008, "If I had a job that needed doing today and Mulcahy were available, I'd pick him. Even if he stepped on a few toes he'd get it done."[4]

Some doubted this, but Herb Jaffe, a highly respected columnist of the state's largest newspaper, the *Star Ledger*, noticed something about Bob: "He brought the portfolio of a brilliant administrator who could handle pressure with calm and provide cool assurance, of a man who knew how to routinely plunge into long hours of work, of one who knew how to turn chaos into order . . . indeed it was time to calculate new plans."[5]

What was to come in the 1980s and 1990s would have been impossible to envision for the dreamers and planners who launched the Meadowlands. An arena would be added that would house the New Jersey Devils and Nets and become a must-stop destination for the top entertainment acts in the world. Giants Stadium, built to lure one football team across the Hudson River, added the New York Jets and became the highest-grossing concert facility in the world.

In one 750-acre patch of reclaimed land in East Rutherford, the sports complex became the only site in the world that was home to five professional sports franchises. In short order, it drew seven games of the FIFA World Cup, a papal visit, and the last NCAA Final Four men's basketball championship played in an arena. A few years after its construction, everyone with a faint interest in sports or entertainment knew about the Meadowlands. It was an international brand.

Left to right: Bob, Brendan Byrne, Harold Hodes, and New Jersey Supreme Court Justice Stewart Pollack at the unveiling of former New Jersey governor Brendan Byrne's statue in front of the Essex County Court House, 2017.

None of this happened in a vacuum. Bob hired and promoted the best and the brightest. His sports management and racing executives went on to build the Meadowlands brand and take on challenges at the highest levels across the industry.

Bob was never afraid of strong, smart personalities disagreeing with him because he had a seemingly lost gift among chief executives today—namely, the awareness of knowing what he didn't know and having the best in place to advise him, not just "yes" him to death. Bob also engendered loyalty. Despite closed-door disagreements, once a decision was made on a course, everyone on his team was on board.

It certainly is one profound measure of a chief executive to chart the subsequent careers of his senior people. By this matrix, Bob's time at the NJSEA was an unmitigated success. The men and women who oversaw the stadium and arena operation, racing, and business development and finance are now at the top of their respective fields.

Patience and foresight are difficult qualities for CEOs to exemplify in a world screaming for immediate results, but Bob saw that much of what was worthy of achieving was going to take time, planning, and relationship building.

Years of staging early round and regional finals of the NCAA men's basketball championship laid the groundwork for achieving a goal that for generations had seemed impossible—the NCAA Final Four, March Madness, was coming to the metropolitan area. Some may have forgotten that New York was off-limits to the old guard of the NCAA due to the National Invitational Tournament (NIT) at Madison Square Garden. That and the organizers' fear that their big event would get lost in New York seemed to make the bid a long shot.

In typical inclusive fashion, Bob oversaw a video pitch to the Site Selection Committee for the Final Four that included a voice-over by legendary Bill Raftery and an eclectic mix of participants, including Governor Tom Kean, Senator Bill Bradley, George Steinbrenner, famous New York restaurateurs, Duke legend Mike Krzyzewski, and even Richard Nixon. (Yes, I know, I had the same immediate reaction, but our college sports guys said the Selection Committee was a very conservative group, and for them, the former president worked.) Incidentally, the chairman of the NCAA Basketball Committee was Jim Delany, the Big Ten commissioner responsible for inviting Rutgers to the Big Ten.

Bob also had the clout with the port authority to ensure that one tube of the Lincoln Tunnel would be held to guarantee on-time travel on game nights from the New York headquarters hotel to the Meadowlands.

The first and only Final Four so far in the region—and the last ever held in an arena—came to East Rutherford in 1996.

Having diplomatic relations with the byzantine empire of the NCAA requires a special level of patience, the ability to conceive and stage big-time events, and a healthy understanding of their institutional respect for the dollar. Bringing truly impactful college football to the Meadowlands centered on the Kickoff Classic.

The strategic vision for the sports complex under Bob and Chairman Hanson, and then carried through by future chairmen like Senator Ray Bateman, was to make the Meadowlands a showplace for the world's biggest events. Its geographic location in the heart of a great consumer marketplace gave the Meadowlands the opportunity, but its top-notch facilities led by the finest operations staff in the country gave it an impeccable industry-wide reputation. During a prior NCAA Regional Final at the then Continental Airlines Arena, I recalled Duke coaching legend Mike Krzyzewski saying in a press conference that the "Meadowlands is a first-class facility. When you come here, all you have to worry about is the game; the operations are handled perfectly."

The NCAA was not the only organization whose politics seemed as byzantine as the Congress of Vienna in 1840. The huge success of the Cosmos and the international friendlies at Giants Stadium set the stage for negotiations with FIFA, the world governing body of soccer, to bring games of the 1994 World Cup to the Meadowlands. Both Governor Jim Florio and George Zoffinger were very helpful.

Fans are hipper these days, but in the early 1990s, Americans generally didn't understand the significance of the World Cup. The world is interested in the Olympics, but it doesn't stop to watch. The streets of Rome and Rio are empty when those nations play in the World Cup. Hosting these games was a building block for the subsequent Women's World Cup, which saw staggering television ratings for U.S. games.

FIFA has a well-earned reputation for arrogance, as recent indictments show. After all, when the Soviet Union broke up the Baltic states, Lithuania, Latvia, and Estonia applied for membership in FIFA before they applied to the United Nations. So of course, negotiating with them was not going to be easy. FIFA had to come to the metropolitan area for at least some of the games. There were a few minor problems for an organization that never needed to compromise. The football field design that served Giants Stadium so well in terms of sightlines was too small for a regulation

World Cup field (not enough sideline or corner kick space). And football games were then being played on artificial turf.

Bob's team came up with an ingenious plan for natural turf that also originally included a deck over the first-row stands to raise the field. He then had to sell the idea to the Giants and Jets, whose stadium would be altered just a few weeks before their preseason began. Thankfully, persuasion reigned, and the installation of natural turf was all that was required. The games themselves were magnificent, topped by Italy-Ireland, a quarterfinal, and a semifinal that billions of people watched worldwide.

Of course, one could overlook FIFA's demand that red carpets be laid down for their officials when the stadium was rocking with the songs and flags of various nations.

There were security concerns leading up to the games. A year earlier, the 1993 World Trade Center bombing had occurred.

Every imaginable international, federal, and state police and security agency was involved. One agency wanted to have a press event prior to the first game in order to parade all the special weaponry and vehicles they had at their disposal as a show of force. Bob quickly rejected that idea. He was more concerned with preparation than scaring the potential fan base.

I know from experience that in its heyday in the 1980s and 1990s, if you told someone you worked at the NJSEA/Meadowlands Sports Complex, they would envision you backstage at glamorous concerts or tossing footballs in the parking lot with Phil Simms.

Hardly. But certainly, satisfaction came to all those working long hours to oversee the various sports, racing, and entertainment events that drew crowds of up to 80,000 people and gave the much-maligned state of New Jersey positive publicity.

The *New York Times* noted in October 1993 that Bob ran the NJSEA "with quiet fervor and foresight that have made it one of the nation's most successful sports and entertainment complexes."[6]

But the job brought crises as well as kudos. Suffice it to say that a few entertainment moguls had interesting definitions of *integrity*.

In the mid-1980s, it was clear that New Jersey's leading thoroughbred racetrack, historic Monmouth Park, was going to be for sale. At that time, a flashy Wall Street financier named Bob Brennan was all the rage in the state. First Jersey Securities commercials featuring him flying around in helicopters were a staple on New York and Philadelphia television.

Brennan was heavily invested in horse racing, with a stud farm in Monmouth County he named Due Process to tweak his frequent government accusers. He also revived Garden State Park in Cherry Hill. His name was on buildings throughout the state. There was just one small drawback: the system found him guilty of multiple financial crimes.

Bob and Chairman Hanson knew before his fall that Brennan taking over Monmouth Park would be a tragedy (and potential death knell) to racing in the state. Convincing the powers in Trenton to allow the NJSEA to purchase Monmouth was no simple matter. After all, this was a public agency buying a private business. Most lament how long it takes to get legislation through a major state senate and assembly—but not this time, and it was not the only time the NJSEA got what it needed quickly. Chairman Jon Hanson called Governor Tom Kean and got the action approved over the phone in 1985. Bob had the relationships with Hanson and Governor Kean as well as the legislative leadership to help get the deal done. Jon Hanson, then and now one of the preeminent figures in New Jersey business and public service, guided the mission while allowing the executives to function.

Today, the thoroughbred horsemen, who may have had nowhere to run after the Brennan empire collapse, operate Monmouth Park for themselves.

From its very germination as an idea in the mind of Governor Bill Cahill, predecessor to Brendan Byrne, the Meadowlands Sports Complex was a favorite whipping boy of some in the New York political and media glitterati (except when they wanted tickets and special treatment for events).

When the plan was announced for the racetrack and stadium in East Rutherford, then New York Governor Nelson Rockefeller jawboned his brother and other Wall Street titans to pull support from the necessary bond sale to fund the project.

Simultaneously, they floated a phony story about New York State getting behind the construction of a new stadium over the rail yards in Sunnyside Queens. Of course, that bond issue never happened, and the stadium was never built. New York believed it was audacious for New Jersey to enter the sports and entertainment big leagues.

In a truly tragic coincidence, four New York Giants players were diagnosed with some form of cancer after 1980. Howard Cosell, who was then at the height of his fame and had pervasive media platforms from which to pontificate, declared that there was a cancer cluster at the Meadowlands. He proclaimed it was not environmentally or medically safe to be there.

Cosell, who like some other New Yorkers couldn't fathom the idea that the Giants and Jets had moved six miles west, were all too happy to perpetuate the disdain for New Jersey. Of course, even in the seemingly more controlled media world of the 1980s, all hell broke loose.

Bob understood immediately that action needed to be taken. Despite the counsel of experts who said that none of the cancers were environmentally related, not only the players and the media but the millions of fans attending events at the complex needed to know the truth from an unassailable source. Bob got that. Cosell might have been a legendary blowhard, but he had a huge audience.

Bob convinced the state and his board to invest in a true independent study conducted by leading cancer experts. Its cost in dollars was substantial, but the truth is priceless. Some in the NJSEA were concerned that they would not control the findings, but that's not how Bob led. Some years later, one of the doctors wrote that he was duly impressed when the only guidance the research team received from Bob was to discover the truth.

Dr. Frederick B. Cohen, director of medical oncology at Newark Beth Israel Hospital, Dr. Paul Lioy, director of exposure measurement and assessment at the University of Medicine and Dentistry of New Jersey, and their teams were engaged and eventually announced the findings of their thorough and complete study in April 1989.

Dr. Cohen was one of five experts who examined the medical histories of all 7,889 people who worked at the complex since it opened in 1976. The investigators also tested the levels of volatile organic compounds, such as benzene, in the air and the level of electromagnetic radiation on the site from nearby radio towers. Dr. Cohen said that the players' cancers had begun long before they came to work for the Giants. He called the cancers a coincidence.

Dr. Paul Lioy said airborne levels of 14 chemical compounds were tested around the site, including the fields used by the players and the backstretch area of the Meadowlands Racetrack. All were within safe limits. In a word, the study was comprehensive.

In a world driven by the media and political and public affairs, Bob's style was to rely on the one thing that would baffle critics: the truth.

The study was front-page news for a day. The incendiary allegations went away. Both the methodology of the study and the integrity of the doctors conducting it were unassailable.

Dealing with professional sports franchise owners could be particularly challenging. The football franchises were owned in Bob's tenure by men of honor, Wellington Mara and Bob Tisch of the New York Giants and Leon Hess of the New York Jets. Both Mr. Hess, who had sat across the table and negotiated a refinery deal with Muammar Gaddafi, and Mr. Mara, a true legend in the NFL, protected their rights and their fans with a passion but at the end of the day would always say that with Bob, a handshake was as solid as a contract.

One year, a horsemen's strike threatened the harness racing meet, the financial lifeblood of the complex. Bob knew the horsemen were in the wrong and did not shirk from calling their bluff. The strike quickly ended, and one participant who is considered the greatest harness racing driver in history said, "I'm glad I don't play poker with Bob every Saturday."

Bob was at a quiet lunch with Terry and longtime friends Richard and Paula Shea at the Black Horse Inn in Mendham one Saturday when his phone started going off about the infamous snowball incident that had just happened at Giants Stadium.

That day, bored and frustrated football fans rained snowballs down on the field and the opposing team. (One of the "gentlemen" taken out of the stands for doing so said, "Everybody was doing it." He was the vice principal of a school, and the stadium head of security asked him how many times he had heard that from students in his office who had been acting like knuckleheads.) There was no greater gentleman in the sports business than then Giants co-owner Wellington Mara. Seeing front-page pictures in the *New York Daily News* of a Giants fan hurling an ice ball at the field broke his heart.

What the fan didn't know was that Bob had a camera system installed for the World Cup so that any troublemaker in the stands could be quickly located. Was it a good day in NJSEA history? Of course not, but the upshot is that it never happened again.

Bob and his team dealt frequently with all types of people at the complex. Sometimes there were awkwardly humorous moments when parents were called to pick up an underage daughter or son at a concert because he or she had been caught with contraband. When the parents arrived, they were often shocked by how their daughters were dressed (e.g., channeling early Madonna). Of course, the girls would leave the house in parent-appropriate outfits, then stop at the turnpike rest area and change.

As safe as the Meadowlands was, parents were still leery of dropping their kids off, especially as the boy band phenomenon exploded. So Bob and his arena people, led by Michael Rowe, came up with an industry-leading idea.

They built a quiet room (lounge) in the arena where parents could wait out the concert if their tweens or young teens were attending. It was a huge hit.

Bob with Meadowlands chairman Jon Hanson before a Kickoff Classic game, early 1980s. Jon and Bob worked on many deals together, including the Jets and Devils coming to the Meadowlands.

The concert business brought great attention to New Jersey due to massive sold-out shows, including the Springsteen phenomenon, but it also brought its share of controversy and, in one case, tragedy.

Sometimes in controversy, Bob would see that his strategy was going to lose, but he went ahead anyway because there was a stand that needed to be taken. In one noteworthy concert case, principle was more important than being right even if it resulted in a loss in federal court and 50,000 kids giving Bob the one-finger salute. An annual event on the stadium concert schedule was the Ozzfest, put together by Ozzy Osbourne of Black Sabbath fame, and it would feature many bands of the heavy metal fringe.

As the 1997 festival approached, concerns were raised by the inclusion of two acts, Pantera and Marilyn Manson. At Pantera's previous shows, fans tore seats apart at the lead singer's urging. Marilyn Manson's self-proclaimed satanic, anti-Christian bent had caused mass controversy across the country. Manson was the flavor of the month for the outrage lovers, and his over-the-top message attracted attention for a while (but ultimately led to a career that is now relegated to "Whatever happened to?" stories).

Outside counsel, the gifted Joel Kobert, made it clear that the Meadowlands would have a hard time prevailing if the promoter sued the NJSEA for trying to have Pantera and Manson removed from the bill.

But Bob felt that sometimes an unpopular, even losing stand was worth taking to make a point. So he took such a stand with the support of a courageous board.

And the Meadowlands lost in federal court as the legendary Floyd Abrams, America's leading First Amendment attorney who had recently won the Larry Flynt Supreme Court case, argued for the promoter that a public venue had no right to ban acts. Abrams prevailed.

The court ordered the show to go on, and Bob's final compliment was Marilyn Manson calling him out from the stage and having 50,000 metalheads flip Bob "the bird" up in the NJSEA suite on Father's Day. You had to be there.

The introduction and growth of casinos in Atlantic City through the late 1970s and 1980s simply devastated the financial underpinning of the NJSEA revenue from horse racing. The great Cahill/Byrne idea of having horse racing revenue pay for the racetrack and Giants Stadium actually worked.

It worked so well that excess revenue was sent to the state. The arena was built. Then the casinos immediately and inexorably eroded racing's bottom line, and governors and legislatures of both parties had bigger concerns than addressing the now not so solvent NJSEA.

Perhaps Jerry Izenberg, the legendary sports columnist for the *Newark Star Ledger*, put it best when he wrote, "Bob Mulcahy remains the only one on the horizon who could take it [the sports complex] to a point that moved it from spectacular novelty to national showpiece."[7]

Governors Byrne, Kean, Florio, and Whitman all relied on him. Chairmen Hyland, Hanson, Levine, Goodman, Francis, and Bateman trusted his judgment. Later at Rutgers, Governors DiFrancesco, McGreevey, and Codey provided crucial support.

Longtime Republican state senator and good friend, Ray Bateman is a great example of bipartisan leadership and farsighted chairing of a major state authority. Governor Byrne's opponent in the 1977 gubernatorial campaign capped his distinguished public service career with his chairmanship of the NJSEA. Did he harbor any resentment because Bob, a Byrne confidant, was the CEO?

No, he forged a working partnership with Bob that steered the NJSEA through some of its most difficult times. Ray became a close personal friend and confidant of Bob's and a tireless advocate for Rutgers.

Serving on multiple corporate and nonprofit boards showed Bob's standing in the community—but perhaps not as much as the list of people who tried to recruit him. The owner's committee also nominated Bob as one of two finalists to become Pete Rozelle's successor as the NFL commissioner.

Major League Baseball came after Bob twice. They once asked him to become the American League president; another time, George Steinbrenner asked him to become the executive vice president of the Yankees. Wall Street called as well with an investment banking partnership. But Bob stayed at the NJSEA.

The *New York Daily News* ranked him sixth in the metropolitan area sports power list, and the *Star Ledger* put Bob second to the governor in New Jersey in their sports power rankings.

In the pages to come, you will read about the decisions—good and bad—and the trials and triumphs that marked Bob's years at Rutgers, but I started this foreword by suggesting that the "how" in Bob's life is more telling than the "what."

Just ask former Rutgers star lineman Shaun O'Hara, a Super Bowl winner as a member of the Giants, whom Bob called more than once to encourage him to finish his degree. Bob never forgot his charges even when they had left the nest, and Shaun gratefully took the advice.

Governor Chris Christie turned to Jon Hanson, head of the Governor's Advisory Commission on New Jersey Gaming, Sports and Entertainment, to tackle the daunting issues facing the future of racing, the future of the sports complex, and the reinvention of Atlantic City.

Bob and Jon's long relationship continued when Chairman Hanson turned to Bob for help on the commission, and the governor appointed him vice chairman of the Casino Reinvestment Development Authority at the most critical juncture in Atlantic City's history. He is now the chairman.

Leadership, management style, and corporate culture are simply clichés or business school course titles unless these qualities manifest in daily decision-making and one-on-one relationships in the workplace.

Accountability is essential to strategic success, yet many CEOs struggle with allowing their lieutenants to lead rather than micromanaging them. Years ago at the NJSEA, the CFO, Jim Durkin, was a crusty but effective financial manager. When I first came on board, I would sit in his office weekly to be brought up to speed on the complicated financing of the organization. Jim kept a noticeably clean desk—save for one red folder. After a few visits, I finally asked what was in that folder. Jim replied, "We have three key financial metrics, and in there are the weekly updates of the three things Bob asks me about every Friday." It is written that faith without works is dead.

On a more personal level, at any stop along the way from Mendham, to Trenton, to the Meadowlands and Rutgers, it is easy to find employees and others whom Bob went beyond the normal bounds to help. Ask his former employees about Bob's successes and you are likely to hear about how he touched their lives. Take the union worker who became a salaried employee with a serious preexisting condition requiring major surgery. "Not covered," said the insurance protocol; "Not for long," said Bob. And covered it was.

Or ask Arnie Wexler, one of the nation's leading advocates for compulsive gamblers, what it meant when Bob quietly overcame the opposition of the racing industry and posted the 800 number for gambling help for the first time on racetrack walls.

Since 2009, Bob has continued the path of public service, from the Governor's Advisory Commission on New Jersey Gaming, Sports and Entertainment, to the chairmanship of the Casino Reinvestment Development Authority, to those missions out of the spotlight, such as being on the board of Atlantic Health System and chairman of the Georgian Court University Board of Trustees. He also serves on the Pinstripe Bowl Committee at the request of the New York Yankees, and in his current home county of Somerset, he has served on the Park Commission Foundation and as a senior adviser to the Somerset Patriots baseball team at the request of its owner and very successful businessman Steve Kalafer.

The personal history recounted in this foreword provided the experience, foresight, wisdom, and integrity necessary for Bob to build the program at Rutgers. Of equal importance, college basketball and football are lost in a morass of cheating scandals, academic fraud, FBI investigations, and distorted priorities. In the closing chapters of the book, Bob leverages his decades of frontline experience to present a way out.

For the sake of full disclosure, I have known Bob well since 1989. I worked at his side at the NJSEA through many long nights of world-class events, traumas, challenges, good ideas bearing fruit, and well-meant ideas that went badly.

Through it all, he maintained one quality that is increasingly rare today, so elusive, and so easy to lose track of: integrity. And there was a day some 29 years ago when a quiet conversation behind closed doors completely changed my life for the better.

John Samerjan

JOHN SAMERJAN served as the vice president of public affairs at the NJSEA under Bob Mulcahy. A former spokesman for Governor Thomas H. Kean and executive director of the New Jersey State Senate, currently he is principal of JStrategies LLC, a public affairs consulting firm, and teaches in the School of Communication and Information at Rutgers, the State University of New Jersey.

PREFACE

This book is part memoir, part policy paper, part homily, and part State of the Athletic Union Address. The rest is a dynamic conversation about college sports—past, present, and future.

I walked into my office as the athletic director (AD) of Rutgers University in 1998 and walked out of it in 2008. However, I have enjoyed maintaining a dedicated presence inside centers of influence that survey all divisions of intercollegiate athletics in America today.

Many years of direct experience and leadership have provided me with insight into the meteoric growth of and controversies surrounding university athletic programs, particularly in football and men's basketball.

Among the organizations I am honored to serve with are the National Football Foundation and College Hall of Fame, the New York Yankees, the Somerset Patriots, and the Atlantic League of Professional Baseball. I am also proud to be a mentor and advisor to ADs and other senior officials directing college-level and professional sports.

There are abundant opportunities today for student athletes to succeed, schools' athletic programs to prosper, and intercollegiate sports to enhance all corners of the American university experience. Meanwhile, serious and systemic difficulties confronting the very integrity of college revenue sports, football and basketball, have created a disturbing perfect storm. This book will explore some of the most pronounced issues.

I felt it was critical to provide the historical background to demonstrate how the success of the Rutgers Athletic program happened. Unfortunately, leadership in today's world seems to forget the role of history in making decisions.

AN ATHLETIC DIRECTOR'S STORY AND THE FUTURE OF COLLEGE SPORTS IN AMERICA

CHAPTER 1

WHY RUTGERS?

It is not out of the question that becoming the Director of Intercollegiate Athletics at Rutgers University was inevitable for me. Looking back on the events leading up to that decade in my life and career, it seemed bound to happen.

Soon after Brendan Byrne was reelected as the governor of New Jersey in 1978, he named me as his chief of staff. During Governor Byrne's first term, Rutgers president Ed Bloustein relentlessly urged the governor to enact a state income tax that would enhance financial support statewide for education.

After the tax was enacted—with great difficulty and by expending a lot of political capital—I was surprised by President Bloustein's callous indifference for Byrne's active support. Bloustein publicly supported New Jersey Senator Ray Bateman, who happened to be my good friend but also Byrne's opponent.

As has been a common theme through the years, once again, Rutgers misplayed its political position and influence in the state of New Jersey.

Following the election, the governor turned to me and said, "Bob, from now on, you deal with Rutgers."

I accepted the challenge and tried to do my best for the governor, the school, and the state of New Jersey. It was a prelude to my association with one of the country's oldest and most distinguished universities.

Following the 1983 football season, Fred Gruninger, Rutgers's athletic director (AD), called me. I wasn't at the statehouse anymore; I was president and CEO of the New Jersey Sports and Exposition Authority (NJSEA). Fred and I had worked together before on NCAA matters, as Rutgers had served as the host institution for a number of Division I Men's Basketball Tournament events at the Meadowlands.

Rutgers had a new financial challenge to solve. This one involved the athletics program. Since I was the state's point man for Rutgers, they called on me again.

The university wanted to hire a new head football coach after firing Frank Burns after 11 seasons. I had great respect for Frank as a coach and for what he accomplished during his tenure with the Scarlet Knights. Burns was a great high school football player in his scholastic days at Rahway, and as a quarterback at Rutgers, he was known as "Flinging Frankie." But while the football schedule began to show significant upgrades in 1977 in pursuit of "bigger-time athletics"—including the likes of Alabama, Tennessee, and Penn State—the facilities and infrastructure remained static. For Coach Burns, it was akin to fighting a nuclear battle with a water pistol.

"We don't have the facilities to draw a topflight coach to central New Jersey," Fred Gruninger told me over the phone. "However, we have a candidate in mind."

I was optimistic about helping him first, the football program second, and Rutgers in the long run. My initial move was to arrange a meeting the next day with Jon Hanson, the chairman of the NJSEA Board of Commissioners; two executive committee members; and representatives from Rutgers. President Bloustein, Fred, and Joe Whiteside, Rutgers's senior vice president for finance, showed up to discuss the situation and their dilemma. It was President Bloustein who had initially recognized the value that intercollegiate athletics could play in raising Rutgers's profile, and he believed that the program could go "bigger-time."

Rutgers needed $5 million just to build its new football training headquarters. Up to this point, the Scarlet Knights had utilized inadequate and antiquated facilities for their athletic training and strength and conditioning programs.

Vaughn McKoy, a former standout defensive back for the Scarlet Knights, offered some insight on the poor facilities at Rutgers he witnessed during a recruiting trip to campus and the football "complex" in early 1986. In his book *Playing Up* (2013), Vaughn describes touring the Rutgers football weight room:

> I couldn't wait to see what a Division I college football weight room looked like. I just knew that Rutgers would have a state-of-the-art weight room filled with free weights, squat machines and leg presses.
>
> We entered the stadium parking area closest to the team's locker room, parked the van, and then climbed out. "We're going to show you the weight room first," one of the coaches announced. We all started walking to a brown shack propped up next to the tennis courts. . . . *No way! This shack cannot be the weight room for a Division I program*, I thought.
>
> The shack measured about twenty by twenty feet and had only one way in and one way out. No free weights, just ten or twelve Nautilus machines, some mirrors, and a few water coolers. This shack did not represent a football program trying to take things to the next level. It made me question Rutgers commitment to big-time football.[1]

We began the process by offering a proposal: the NJSEA would loan Rutgers $1.5 million if the university could find the other $3.5 million. As I would come to realize was the norm rather than the exception, Rutgers said it was hard-pressed for money and insisted it could not raise the $3.5 million.

Jon Hanson and I looked at each other. We both were accustomed to finding creative financial options. At the time, Jon and I had worked together for five years, planning and negotiating partnerships that brought professional sports, economic development, businesses and jobs, and millions of fans to the state.

Rutgers football coach Frank Burns and Bob discussing the Garden State
Bowl, December 1981.

The New Jersey Devils were playing hockey and the New Jersey Nets were shooting hoops in the Meadowlands, which was also the site of sold-out concerts and the game that would become college football's premier preseason event, the Kickoff Classic. Giants Stadium in the Meadowlands was home to the New York Giants and the New York Jets of the NFL. And Jon, among the most experienced business leaders and strategists around, was a trusted partner. We suggested asking the state of New Jersey for the additional $3.5 million.

President Bloustein and Gruninger wondered if we really could pull it off. Jon revealed his answer that night when he called Governor Tom Kean, who had succeeded Brendan Byrne. Twenty-four hours later, the governor announced a $5 million project to build two new athletic facilities at Rutgers. These upgrades resulted in the original Hale Center, the football headquarters and training facility attached to the east side of Rutgers Stadium, and the yearlong indoor practice facility affectionately known as the "Bubble." And yes, Rutgers finally had a weight room that was on par with many of its eastern rivals. The state offered $3.5 million, and $1.5 million came from the NJSEA.

Standing next to Governor Kean was Dick Anderson, who at the time was a highly respected assistant football coach at Penn State. Anderson agreed to become the new head football coach at Rutgers, contingent on the commitment of the facility upgrades.

We told Rutgers we could do it and that we would do it, and we got it done.

Five years passed, and Rutgers still had my number on speed dial. Doug Graber, a successful NFL assistant, had replaced Dick Anderson as the Scarlet Knights' head coach. Unfortunately, Dick was unable to lead Rutgers to the annual winning seasons and bowl bids he was a proud part of achieving under Joe Paterno at Penn State. He recruited quality student athletes with character and was a good coach—especially in big games—but once again, he did not have the facilities and budget necessary to compete at the level Rutgers aspired to. Rutgers had made considerable strides with the Hale

Center and the Bubble five years earlier, but in college football, upgrading facilities is a constant task. Rutgers was playing its home games in an aging 23,000-seat stadium that hadn't seen any improvements in more than five decades.

Not being able to put a consistent winner on the field was not all Coach Anderson's fault. But at the end of the day, right or wrong, the success of a college football coach is in large part measured by Ws and Ls.

In my opinion, Rutgers did not give him enough time or support. But Coach Anderson did run the kind of program the university should have been proud of. He also gave Greg Schiano, who later became the most successful head football coach (in terms of program administration and bowl game championships) in Rutgers history, the opportunity to be a graduate assistant and gain a unique knowledge of the ins and outs of Rutgers, something that would come in handy during his tenure, which began in December 2000.

Coach Graber came to see me. Rutgers needed a new football stadium badly. It had a Depression-era, decaying, not-ready-for-prime-time facility with wooden bleachers and weeds growing in between the seats. Its best playing days were clearly over.

If Rutgers wanted to compete in the upper echelons of Division I football, a huge improvement was needed. The open-air press box was outdated, and the coaching boxes were nonexistent. The university simply could not host Saturday night college football games in a stadium that was ready for retirement. ESPN once asked Rutgers if the network could broadcast the Pitt game. Rutgers had no lights and was forced to rent them to get national TV exposure, all the while putting its aged, inadequate facility on display for the entire nation to see. I remember the night well, as I watched the game from the roof of the Hale Center—that was the early version of the stadium's "club" level, I guess.

Meanwhile, the NJSEA was restructuring its debt service, which was a process the state legislature had to approve. Around the time Coach Graber came to see me to explain his dilemma at Rutgers, the state treasurer asked me if the NJSEA had any interest in being part of building a convention center in Atlantic City. The projected cost was $271 million.

I told him I had an idea how all of it could work: What if legislators sponsored a bill that would restructure the NJSEA's debt and build Rutgers a new stadium? In addition, what if they built a soccer and lacrosse stadium and a track-and-field facility as well as break ground for a convention center in Atlantic City?

This option offered attractive assets for all three parts of the state—north, central, and south.

Tip O'Neill, the one-time powerful Speaker of the House, said that all politics are local. He practiced that philosophy throughout his eminent career of public service. I will always remember having coffee and talking politics with him at his home on Cape Cod on a summer Saturday morning. Our conversation was arranged through my relationship with Tip's son Tommy, the lieutenant governor of Massachusetts.

Governor Byrne also knew how to maneuver in political mazes, and he taught me a few things along the way. I relied on those tactics to assist both Rutgers and the NJSEA, my two main priorities.

The business of politics inevitably presents difficulties, and this time was no exception. New Jersey Governor Jim Florio, who had succeeded Tom Kean, told me he could not publicly endorse the bill. But if it was passed and came to his desk, he would sign it. I called former governors Byrne and Kean and asked them for support. They agreed, and their consensus provided vital bipartisan backing.

Then in the assembly's final lame duck session on a cold January night in 1992, as midnight approached, the bill was the last one on the docket. I worked the room with Harold Hodes, my successor as chief of staff in the statehouse, along with the late Cary Edwards, a former state attorney general and counsel to the governor. Both men were longtime friends and veteran public leaders in the state.

We pressured Joseph Doria, the Speaker of the Assembly, to put the bill up for a vote. Meanwhile, I refused to speak with Bob Janiszewski, the Hudson County executive, because he was trying to hold the bill up for some compromise. Finally we persuaded the Speaker to put the bill up. It passed, and Rutgers "miraculously" found the money to build a new football stadium.

Rutgers was not in my daily thoughts in 1997 as I finished my 19th year running the NJSEA, although the Scarlet Knights did play periodically at Giants Stadium. But now I was about to be associated with Rutgers again.

At a birthday celebration for Jon Hanson at the Somerset Hills Country Club, I struck up a conversation with Tony Cicatiello, one of Jon's friends who also served on Rutgers's Board of Governors. We talked about Rutgers athletics and its primary woes: lackluster financial support, limited participation from alumni, and inability to compete in the NCAA's Division I revenue sports of football and men's basketball. Women's basketball, conversely, had a tradition of doing considerably better, having won the 1982 Association for Intercollegiate Athletics for Women (AIAW) basketball championship.

Then Tony asked me a question: Would I ever be interested in becoming the director of intercollegiate athletics at Rutgers?

I knew that Gruninger and the athletics program received constant criticism from the New Jersey media, influential people across the state, and an increasing number of loyal alumni and fans. Notwithstanding Fred's long and faithful service to the school, too many years of losing seasons in the major sports had many people convinced that things had to change.

At the same time, George Steinbrenner, proud owner of what many consider the greatest franchise in major league sports history, the New York Yankees, asked me to come and work for him as the executive vice president. George and I had been good friends for many years.

It was a once-in-a-lifetime offer for anyone who dreamed of working for and with one of America's most honored and traditional sports enterprises. Meanwhile, Tony Cicatiello's idea also appealed to me, though I wasn't sure why. It was just that it did, and I was not about to dismiss the idea outright.

Left to right: New Jersey Senate president Don DiFrancesco, Bob, New Jersey state treasurer Brian Clymer, Rutgers University president Fran Lawrence, Rutgers AD Fred Gruninger, and New Jersey governor Jim Florio at the ground breaking for the new Rutgers football stadium in Piscataway, 1992.

I decided to confront my situation the same way I often handled important events in my life and my career—by talking things over with people I trusted. They would tell me what they believed, and I knew it would be the truth.

My wife, Terry, and I and our two youngest daughters, Megan and Deidre, went out to dinner. We got right to the point. Both opportunities were attractive. I certainly would not be bored at either job, and I knew it. There would be new and interesting challenges either way.

Finally, one of my daughters could tell I was leaning toward Rutgers, and she asked why. I said something appealed to me about working with student athletes who might be more interested in competing for the love of the game than for contracts and money. Terry felt the same way, and Rutgers would be a change from professional sports.

I also knew that many of the university's best high school athletes chose to compete for programs outside of New Jersey rather than staying home and playing for the Scarlet Knights. I was drawn to serving in a leadership position—even one with built-in risks and challenges—where I could reverse a long and embarrassing pattern for the school's athletic teams, especially its flagship sports.

Up to that time, my whole life was spent in New Jersey. This was a chance to help Rutgers earn national prominence. In my heart, I knew this could be a difficult undertaking. Still, I felt drawn to do it because I had a chance to create something remarkable.

First, I told George Steinbrenner my decision and thanked him for honoring me with his offer and his trust. He understood and wished me luck, and we remained friends for the rest of his days.

Early in 1998, Tony Cicatiello convinced Governor Christie Whitman to intervene with Rutgers president Francis Lawrence during the search for the new AD. On April 15, 1998, I was introduced as the next AD of Rutgers University.

After all that happened—from the day Ed Bloustein supported Ray Bateman over Governor Byrne to Tony Cicatiello's question—perhaps it was foreseeable that Rutgers would become the next major challenge and assignment awaiting me.

John McLaughlin, a columnist at the *Star Ledger*, wrote a far-sighted column following my farewell party at the NJSEA. Rereading John's column over the years, I've often appreciated his ability to judge who I was and what I did at the Meadowlands and then foresee some of the trials I would find at Rutgers:

> There were horse people there. Football, basketball, and hockey and soccer people. Three governors. Judges and journalists. Priests and politicians.

Legislators, lobbyists, labor leaders, lawyers. Some 450 of them, to bid farewell after 19 years to Bob Mulcahy, President and CEO of the New Jersey Sports and Exposition Authority.

The much-revered Mulcahy has transferred his talents from East Rutherford to New Brunswick, where he has been entrusted with resuscitating a moribund and money-losing Rutgers University athletic program.

It is the football team that's the problem. You can turn a basketball program around by recruiting two or three blue chippers a year. Football's harder. And it is Mulcahy's job to do what it takes to turn a $3 million annual athletic department deficit into a bit of a profit.

[This evening] he made clear that the one attribute he values most in his colleagues is loyalty. He may find that he won't find much of that at Rutgers; and that handshake deals don't cut it there. At Rutgers he'll have to cope with the passions of self-righteous faculty and alumni who believe that the de-emphasis of athletics will lead axiomatically to beefing up academics.

At Rutgers Mulcahy will be up against a well-organized group whose agents will work hard to see that he fails. They call themselves the Rutgers 1000 and they are determined to block what they see as a trend toward "professionalized college athletics."

For nearly 20 years Bob Mulcahy set a standard for survival in a high-pressure, high-profile, high-paying job that all sorts of connected people wanted for themselves. He is very good at his work, and even better at the politics of it.

A Mulcahy associate who has been around the track a few times himself says: "A lifetime in Trenton, Albany, New York City, or Washington just isn't enough to prepare you for the politics of a modern campus."

Looking back, John McLaughlin was right. With a mandate to fix football and reorganize the athletic department, the decade that followed would test me many times in different ways.

Bob; his wife, Terry; Bob and Terry's seven children; and executive assistant
Carol Baran gathered at Bob's farewell party at the Meadowlands, April 1998.

Some challenges I saw coming, others I did not. But I met every test
with the same principles that guided my judgment up to that time as a
naval officer, New Jersey State Commissioner of Corrections, Chief of
Staff for Governor Byrne, President and CEO of the NJSEA, and a member
on several corporate boards.

Fairness in all of my personal and professional dealings was a principle
in which I firmly believed and always have. At Rutgers, my commitment to
this ideal included the following:

- fairness in building a family atmosphere at work and positive
  chemistry within my staff,
- readiness to listen and understand situations before making decisions that I knew could and would affect people and organizations
  years later, and
- measuring my actions and words by the same standards I expected
  of those who worked alongside me.

I've always had an emotional tie to Rutgers. You don't work seven days a week trying to accomplish something for the state of New Jersey—and for the people of Rutgers—without having emotional ties.

The challenges that awaited me at Rutgers were often exciting, sometimes frustrating, and usually demanding. Most of all, the accomplishments I achieved were very rewarding personally and professionally. My experiences prior to Rutgers prepared me well for the journey I was starting.

CHAPTER 2

ON THE WAY
TO RUTGERS

A large part of my life and my work has revolved around sports in both real and symbolic ways.

Long before I arrived at Rutgers University as the AD, I put on a football uniform for Millburn High School in New Jersey. That was one of my earliest experiences with teamwork, determination, and believing in something larger than myself.

We had a great young football coach, Frank Close, who related to the team and really imparted the lessons of football. He taught us to take the good with the bad because everything we do in life has both. He also taught us how to walk away when the game was over, knowing we had done our best and ready to face whatever came next.

My diverse experiences before becoming a major college AD uniquely prepared me to deal with the countless problems I needed to understand and solve at Rutgers. My career in government, and particularly 19 years at the helm of the NJSEA, provided a broad mix of experiences and contacts. I felt confident in my ability to negotiate and lead Rutgers out of the bottom of Division I intercollegiate athletics and to the national recognition it had sought for decades.

After graduating from Villanova University in 1958, where I was a part of the naval ROTC program, I was commissioned as an ensign in the U.S. Navy.

Bob playing center (91) for Millburn High School with the old-style slap-on helmets, 1953. Notice the single-wing formation used at that time!

I experienced firsthand the purpose of setting a course with clear directions. You need to know where you're going before you get under way.

My time as a division officer aboard two aircraft carriers, being responsible for 40 sailors, plus my role as both prosecutor and defense counsel for special court-martial afforded me insight about supervising people and modeling a naval officer's best and fair conduct.

I learned it was important to stand up for principles and values even when the rules in place seem to say otherwise.

Serving in the navy also provided great experiences in leadership. Being responsible for other men and understanding their problems taught me a lot—and very quickly.

I will always remember the time I served as both prosecutor and defense counsel for a special court-martial panel. As military defense counsel, I could request the court to peremptory dismiss any senior officer on a trial panel.

Under the Uniformed Code of Military Justice, the maximum sentences those courts handed out were six months in prison, six months at hard labor, and dishonorable discharges—all tough punishments.

One particular case, in which I represented a black defendant, left a
deep impression on me. It happened between 1958 and 1960, when seg-
regation was still rooted firmly in many areas of American society and
everyday life.

I knew how some senior officers felt by the racial comments they
made in the wardroom. I also understood that my only choice was to dismiss those particular officers from the case. However, I had to face them
later when we sat down to dinner, and they asked me why I did it. I told
them—respectfully yet firmly. It was an important lesson in maturity and
sensitivity that I carried throughout my life.

Serving in the military is one of the greatest opportunities to develop
character. You learn quickly how great leaders do not need to order others
to follow them. They practice a life of honesty and ethics that others follow
without direct orders.

There isn't necessarily any preparation for managing a real and monumental crisis. Though I trained in the profession of war as a naval officer, the United States operated in peacetime conditions when I joined the
navy's fleet.

We did not see combat, but we were never idle. Serving in peacetime
means being prepared for threats to the nation's security from enemies
known and unknown. We were engaged in antisubmarine surveillance in
the Atlantic and were on duty off Cape Kennedy before and during the
first lunar probe.

After my military commission ended, I returned home to Morristown,
New Jersey, for two years before moving to Mendham, where Terry and I
raised our family. I went to work for the family home building business
with my brother John. Subsequently, our brother, Bill, joined us. After I left
the business in 1974 to go into full-time government service, John ran the
company and became a distinguished builder who won many awards. Bill
followed me into public service and then into the private sector, where he
led a very successful career.

Following service in local government for more than a decade, including, three and half years as a municipal mayor, I was appointed as deputy commissioner of the Department of Institutions and Agencies by Commissioner Ann Klein in 1974. I was responsible for the daily operations of all the mental hospitals, schools for the disabled, the prison system, the welfare system, the Medicaid system, and youth and family services. It was an opportunity to understand firsthand the issues that affect marginalized populations.

As deputy commissioner, I dealt with the tough culture of correctional institutions, including riots at Trenton State Prison. Difficulties in the prison system caused the governor and the legislature to create a separate Department of Corrections. The governor then appointed me to serve as the first Commissioner of Corrections in the state of New Jersey in 1976.

Those experiences presented valuable insight into so much—sometimes too much—of the harshness that exists in the world and our society.

Ten days after my appointment and at a time long before email, text messages, and cell phones, I came home from a high school football game to Terry greeting me at the door with a startling announcement. Prisoners were holding a woman hostage in the sex offenders' unit at Rahway State Prison. I called Jim Stabile, my press officer, and met him at Morristown Airport.

The New Jersey State Police sent a helicopter to pick us up, and we flew to Rahway Prison. I spent the next several hours working to restore a semblance of order to an extremely dangerous situation there. I also knew in a very short time that I could not cave to the prisoners' demands.

At one point, a state police captain came to me and said, "We have a sharpshooter in position. How do you feel about killing the inmate?" I walked down the hall and I said to myself, *Dear God, what am I doing?* Then I turned around, walked back, and told the captain, "I'll negotiate this," which I did without making any dangerous concessions to inmates. No lives were lost.

Each prison incident was a crisis of significant magnitude and danger. I say that without any exaggeration. They happened suddenly, and someone had to make life-or-death decisions from the time they started until they ended. Those decisions were ultimately my responsibility.

Each event represented a personal and professional lesson about making choices based on one's moral values.

Those experiences toughened me for every future crisis I managed in my personal and professional life, but that didn't mean the challenges awaiting me in the years ahead would necessarily be easier to handle, with less tension and fewer consequences. Every one of those also tested my will and my values.

When the hostage crisis at Rahway State Prison was resolved without anyone dying, I never doubted my determination to face anything like it again and come out the other end confident I made the right choices. I then asked the New York Police Department Hostage Team, regarded as the best in the world, to come to New Jersey and train our people.

My service as the Commissioner of Corrections also involved the imprisonment of Joanne Chesimard, a member of the Black Liberation Army, who was charged with murdering a New Jersey State Trooper in cold blood while he performed his sworn duties. What Chesimard and her accomplices did on that tragic route along the New Jersey Turnpike is still an open and sickening memory for many who were there at the time.

Chesimard was captured, tried, and sent to prison after being found guilty of a number of crimes. She escaped from prison in 1979 (after my term as corrections commissioner had ended) and has remained in exile in Cuba for more than 30 years.

After my tenure in the navy and during my career in government, comparisons to sports existed everywhere. Politics in its worst form is a blood sport that only gets you short-time victories and long-term enemies. Ongoing success is earned, and good reputations are built when you let your opponents get back up after a loss with their dignity intact. It's the easiest way to develop mutual respect among people with different points of view—sometimes very different. And the art of real negotiation is a continuous learning process.

The most successful leaders understand that the person you took on yesterday could be the same one you need supporting your position tomorrow. Diplomacy and compromise are all about getting other people to want what you want even though they don't see it that way at first.

My time as Governor Brendan Byrne's chief of staff granted me connections within the leadership of the legislature and across New Jersey's power structure.

At the beginning of Governor Byrne's second term, he and his cabinet agreed on a vision to accomplish. My responsibility was to make sure the cabinet officers adhered to it and to get the program and policies enacted. I already knew that working with politicians required enormous tact.

I took particular pride in three pieces of legislation among the many I worked on. The first and probably the most significant was the passage of the Pinelands Protection Act. It preserved about 20 percent of New Jersey, spanning multiple counties in the state's southern half.

Passing legislation has been compared to making sausage. That analogy held up well in this case.

Governor Byrne and his team had a solid strategy that started with an executive order. We also expected it would be challenged in the courts. Our strategy was to pass the bill in the State Senate first because we had the votes. The toughest part was getting it through the assembly. Developers and others were suing us, and we were concerned about getting the bill passed.

On a Thursday, I got a call from Richard Coffee, the state Democratic chairman and also the executive director of the State Assembly. He said on Monday there would be a motion to recommit the Pinelands bill back to committee for amendment. Allowing that to happen would almost ensure the measure would never pass. Coffee also told me they had the votes to recommit the bill for amendment but not enough to pass it. In effect, the bill would be dead on arrival if it was recommitted to committee.

Along with Harold Hodes, my brilliant strategic deputy, I figured out a plan over the weekend that would lead to the bill's passage, not its defeat. Hodes and I called assembly members to determine their position, as we needed to assess how many votes we had and how many we needed to defeat returning the bill to committee for amendment. A few wanted to vote for the bill if it came up. They were torn between supporting the environment and their responsibility to send it back to committee because of commitments they had made to various constituencies. We asked a few of those if they would stay home while the bill was debated, then promised to bring them back to vote for the Pinelands. Five of them agreed.

With this strategy, we felt we had a five or six vote margin to defeat the motion to recommit.

On Monday morning when I got to the office, Chief Justice Richard Hughes asked to see me about some personnel matters. I went to his office, and he got to the point fast. Justice Hughes asked if we were going to pass the Pinelands bill that day. I told him where we stood. He said, "Here's the number for the phone next to my bed. Call me at any hour because it will make Justice [Morris] Pashman's job a lot easier tomorrow."

I went back and told Governor Byrne the story. "If we don't pass it," I said, "the court will go against us." A group of developers had initiated legal action, saying the state did not have the right to preserve the land via executive order, and Justice Pashman would be writing the decision. That night, the debate went on until approximately 2:00 a.m.

Christopher Jackman, the Speaker of the Assembly, called me and said that a motion to recommit was made in the chamber. It was defeated by the margin of votes that we had converted over the weekend. I asked the speaker for a two-hour recess.

Michael Rowe, one of my bright young aides, was responsible for coordinating the transportation. He sent the state police to pick up the absentee members and return them to the House. Somewhere between 4:00 and 5:00 a.m., we passed the Pinelands Protection Act, thus preventing some 1.1 million acres from becoming strip malls and parking lots.

Other examples of legislative bills my team and I managed to pass include the Administrative Law Judge bill, which created a system to take cases out of the judicial system and allowed them to be handled more efficiently at the administrative level, and the New Jersey Transit Bus Takeover bill, among many others. It was a time of real accomplishment, and I was proud of my part in it.

The opportunity to serve and work alongside Governor Brendan Byrne in four different roles of senior administration was among the most worthwhile periods of my career and my life. I learned so much about the true workings of government, doing the people's business the right way, and working effectively with many different personalities and situations.

Things were about to change in a huge way for me one day in August 1979. I walked into the governor's office with my sandwich in hand to have lunch with him. He was there with former state attorney General Bill Hyland, who was now the chairman of the NJSEA. Governor Byrne laughed when I entered and said, "We just talked about you. We just learned that the third CEO in three years is leaving the sports authority for another job, and I don't need more political pressure for the appointment. If you're willing to go up there and run it, I will name you tomorrow."

That night I went to dinner with Governor Byrne, Harold Hodes, and Jerry English, the governor's legislative counsel. We discussed my going to the Meadowlands and running the NJSEA. I had to decide then and there whether this was the right move for my family and me.

I had visions of running for governor in 1981. This was different, though. It was an opportunity to participate in one of the two passions I had in life: public service and the many opportunities one could find in managing the businesses of professional and intercollegiate sports. And with a growing family, there was the added benefit of an increase in salary.

When Governor Byrne asked me to take the reins as president and CEO of the NJSEA, I knew I was in for an amazing experience. With a terrific team behind me for 19 years, we achieved a vision that others thought was impossible. We turned 750 acres of reclaimed land, much of it previously thought unusable, in northern New Jersey into a dynamic sports and entertainment complex supporting five professional sports franchises. There we also held sold-out concerts by legendary entertainers and artists, a papal visit, and the last NCAA Final Four men's basketball championship played in an arena.

One of the most difficult assignments was also quite personal and heartbreaking for me. It happened years later when then Governor Christie Todd Whitman ordered Brendan Byrne's name removed from the Meadowlands Arena wall. As CEO of the NJSEA, I had to carry that order out. Governor Byrne and I met for breakfast at the legendary Pal's Cabin in West Orange, a haunt of Babe Ruth's and a lifetime favorite of Governor Byrne's. I delivered Whitman's demeaning decision to my former boss, an assignment I did not relish and did not believe in.

I will always believe that Governor Byrne's exceptional service as New Jersey's chief executive officer during a challenging period of economic distress deserves praise from all politically partisan corners of the state. For a Republican incumbent governor to remove his name from the arena building just because he was a Democrat—and because the Whitman administration wanted to sell the naming rights—was petty politics. I thought Governor Whitman's decision made her look bad. A fellow governor deserved more respect than that, especially since he had the courage, against all political advice, to stand up to New York by asking several New Jersey banks, including the Prudential Insurance Company, to support the state and buy bonds when the New York financial community refused, hoping to sink the Meadowlands.

Ironically, the first chairman and CEO of the NJSEA was David A. "Sonny" Werblin, a prominent entertainment executive and Rutgers grad who was also an owner of the NFL's New York Jets and later the chairman of Madison Square Garden.

Many experiences at the Meadowlands directly prepared me for Rutgers.

Our negotiations to bring sports franchises to New Jersey—the New York Jets, the New Jersey Devils, and the New Jersey Generals, later owned

Left to right: Sports announcers Bill Raftery and Don Criqui, Bob, and
Meadowlands chairman Michael Francis discussing betting strategies at the
Kentucky Derby, 1990s.

by renowned entrepreneur and future presidential candidate Donald
Trump—were truly memorable accomplishments.

We did not attempt to replace or upstage Madison Square Garden;
rather, we wanted to be the best we could be and establish our mark as a
sports and entertainment giant and destination. Our forte was hosting big-
time special events, and we did so with great aplomb, better than anyone.

Horse racing enthusiasts soon knew that the Meadowlands sponsored the
greatest harness racing track in the world. We hosted the world's top entertainment acts—including Sinatra, Springsteen, and the Jackson 5—and set
numerous attendance records. We made a big splash in college sports with
the Kickoff Classic, hosting marquee college basketball Top 25 matchups,
and serving as the home of the Seton Hall Pirates and many NCAA Men's
Basketball Tournament contests, culminating with the Final Four in 1996.

It was my privilege to serve in a leadership capacity on both thoroughbred and harness racing industry boards. Every year at the Kentucky

Derby, the Meadowlands entertained the country's top racing media with a dinner that was also attended by our governor.

Most of all, the sports and business relationships I forged, and the numerous deals I brokered while leading the sports complex, were some of the best experiences any AD running a major university sports program could have before setting foot on a college campus and successfully leading a big-time Division I program.

Finally, among the various boards and directorships on which I was proud to serve was the National Football Foundation (NFF) and College Football Hall of Fame. I was a board member for 21 years, starting in 1990. During that time, I served as the hall's Awards Committee chairman for 15 years.

I was shocked to learn that Paul Robeson, a distinguished student and All-American football player at Rutgers University who later became a preeminent singer, actor, and activist in the first half of the 20th century, was not in the College Football Hall of Fame.

His career on and off the field certainly justified it, but the votes were not there. Some individuals objected to Robeson's philosophies and positions on domestic and international affairs.

I was about two votes short of getting a majority to place his name on the ballot. I asked Jon Hanson, then the Hall of Fame's chairman, to expand the committee by two or three members who were more open-minded on the issue. That's how we got Paul Robeson—and then later the legendary Syracuse University and Cleveland Browns all-time great Jim Brown—into the Hall of Fame.

One unfortunate situation during my efforts to induct Paul Robeson and Jim Brown involved two prominent national board members who attacked the vote. They eventually resigned. During that time, I knew getting Paul Robeson elected into the College Football Hall of Fame was the right thing to do.

Among the many events that took place at the Meadowlands and helped prepare me for my time at Rutgers, four stand out: creating the Kickoff Classic, staging the iconic Army-Navy Game, working with the NCAA to

host several NCAA Men's Basketball Tournament Regional Championships, and hosting the Final Four in 1996.

The Kickoff Classic

The Kickoff Classic developed after we decided to close down the Garden
State Bowl. Rutgers had appeared in the inaugural Garden State Bowl in
1978 after a 9–2 regular season, and on a warm (for December) afternoon,
they gave national power Arizona State quite a battle before falling late,
34–18. But we had difficulties getting good teams to commit for the event
in the Northeast in early December. Except for the Rose Bowl, conference
tie-ins for bowl games did not exist like the ones there are today. At the
same time, the NFF and College Hall of Fame was looking for financial
support and wanted to sponsor an early season classic.

We put together a bid. The NCAA sanctioned it, and it benefited the
Hall of Fame and the National Coaches Association as well as the National
Association of Collegiate Directors of Athletics (NACDA), led by the legendary Mike Cleary. We were willing to do something other applicants did
not want to do—guarantee TV revenues for them to share.

The first game, in late August 1983, was a resounding success. It pit-
ted defending national champion Penn State and their iconic coach Joe
Paterno against preseason number-one Nebraska, led by another legend,
Tom Osborne, in front of more than 71,000 fans. Topflight programs such
as Alabama, Ohio State, the University of Southern California, and Florida
State appeared in the game over its 20-year history. Unfortunately, the
classic was forced to come to an end in 2002, although it went out with
a bang when Notre Dame defeated Maryland before nearly 73,000 fans.

The game was such an achievement that many other charities attempted
to duplicate it. But as so often happens after success, there were too many
efforts to do the same thing. The NCAA decided to abolish the waiver for
an extra regular-season game, thus ending the reign of a game that had set
a standard of excellence at the start of the college football campaign.

The Army-Navy Game

One of America's great fall spectacles, the Army-Navy Game, was traditionally played in Philadelphia, with one exception: the year it went to
Pasadena. As with the Kickoff Classic, three years of building relationships
with Carl Ulrich, the AD at Army, and Jack Lengyel, the AD at Navy, paid
off when they agreed to move the game from Philly to the Meadowlands
for one year.

In the process, we had to fend off Philly's Congressman William Gray,
the powerful chairman of the House Budget Committee and a member
of the House Appropriations Committee, which the service academies
had to pay close attention to. We were able to secure the help of New Jersey Senators Bill Bradley and Nick Brady, who neutralized Congressman
Gray. And three more Army-Navy spectacles were played at the Meadowlands thanks in no small part to our initial success with one of America's
all-time great college football classics.

We also created an important and first-time moment by inviting the
top-ranking officials of both service academies to attend the dinner at
the Pegasus Restaurant before the game. From that moment on, a new
and positive camaraderie existed each year leading up to the Army-
Navy Game.

The Final Four

Years of staging early round and regional finals of the NCAA Men's Basketball Tournament laid the groundwork for an honor that many thought
was impossible—securing the NCAA Final Four.

The culmination of the NCAA's March Madness came to the New
York–New Jersey metropolitan area in 1996, and once again, Rutgers University served as the host school. Both the Kickoff Classic and the Final
Four required a strong relationship with the NCAA. (Another forewarn-
ing of my future—the Rutgers connection came forth again when we

designated Rutgers as the host school despite the fact that its Big East rival, Seton Hall, called the Meadowlands home.)

Other Opportunities to Benefit the Garden State

There were many additional opportunities to do things for New Jersey along the way. For example, at Governor Brendan Byrne's request, former U.S. Treasury Secretary and Senator Nick Brady, NJSEA member Bill Taggart, Frank Hartmann, and I flew to Atlanta in 1981. We made a presentation to the U.S. Golf Association (USGA) and proposed they move their headquarters to Basking Ridge, New Jersey. They eventually agreed to our proposal and later built additional facilities.

Another opportunity came up when I served as a member of Governor Richard Codey's commission to set a steroid drug policy for New Jersey high school's interscholastic championships. While it only involved championships, the policy recognized that steroid use presented a genuine danger to scholastic athletes.

In later years, the board of the USGA threatened to move some operations to Rhode Island. The governor at the time, Jim Florio, called me to get the move canceled, and it was.

At one time, Governor Tom Kean asked the NJSEA to take over a long-stalled proposal to build an aquarium in Camden. We did that too. We worked through the difficult maze of Camden County politics with the help of the late senator Walter Rand.

When we built the Byrne Arena, we configured it to accommodate an NHL hockey team as well as the NBA's Brooklyn Nets. However, there was a large obstacle to deal with: the New York Rangers hockey team owned territorial veto rights over the arena area. One day Sonny Werblin, president and CEO of Madison Square Garden, called and asked to meet with me immediately.

Paramount, the motion picture company, owned the Garden at the time. When we sat down, Sonny said, "Paramount gave me permission to move the New York Knicks and the Rangers to New Jersey."

I said, "Sonny, you know that won't happen. Plus, we have a long-term lease with the New Jersey Nets."

I asked him what his real objective was. He said he was having trouble negotiating a tax abatement with the city of New York. I suggested we give the Rangers a six-month option to negotiate a move to New Jersey in return for vacating their veto power over an NHL franchise coming to New Jersey—with a significant payment to us for the option.

We signed the agreement quickly, clearing the way for the New Jersey Devils hockey team to come to New Jersey and for the NHL to establish a new franchise in the state.

In 1981, when the New York Jets played their preseason games in Giants Stadium because the New York Mets were still playing baseball at Shea Stadium in August in Queens, I stopped in to say hello to Leon Hess, who also owned Jets. It was before an exhibition game at the stadium.

Leon Hess asked me, "Would you give me the same benefits the Giants have if I would consider moving the Jets to New Jersey?" I had to figure out quickly how to answer his question while protecting the Giants' exclusive rights at the same time. I definitely wanted to get the Jets to come to New Jersey. "The Sports Authority is willing to give all the rights to the Jets that the Giants now have that were not exclusively granted to the Giants" was my answer.

Thus began three years of negotiations among Jon Hanson; Leon Hess; Steve Gutman, the president of the Jets franchise; and myself. In the end, the Jets, the Giants, and the NJSEA accomplished something that no other NFL team franchise had done before: two NFL teams played in the same stadium. To avert a potential identity crisis, when the Jets played home games at Giants Stadium, the TV networks referred to the facility as "the Meadowlands."

A major obstacle occurred during the second year of negotiations. I was attending a funeral and stepped out to receive a message from Leon Hess, who said it was critical that Jon Hanson and I meet him in New York for lunch. We got together at the legendary La Caravalle restaurant.

During that meeting, Leon described the pressure New York City was putting on him. He suggested giving the New York Jets the option to move

Left to right: New Jersey governor Tom Kean and Bob sensing victory for the Giants on their way to Super Bowl XXI, 1987.

their team to New Jersey for a nonrefundable amount of $5 million. Then Jon said $10 million, and Leon agreed. Our rationale was that we needed the large sum of money to show elected officials in New York City and New Jersey that both sides were serious.

All major actions by the NJSEA required the governor's approval. Leon Hess had not had the pleasure of meeting Governor Kean yet. Jon reached the governor on the phone and introduced Leon, and the two of them had a 45-minute conversation. With Governor Kean's support and approval, we executed the option Leon Hess wanted that afternoon at the restaurant.

Subsequently, both the city of New York and the NJSEA submitted bids to the Jets, and the rest is history. This arrangement, with two NFL teams playing home games in the same venue, helped pave the way for the present-day MetLife Stadium, which replaced Giants Stadium in 2010. Both teams not only play in New Jersey but also have their headquarters, administrative offices, and practice facilities in the Garden State.

The last game the Jets played with Leon as the owner and in attendance was a playoff game against Jacksonville in 1998, a 34–24 victory. Like Wellington Mara of the New York Giants, Leon Hess was a giant of a man. His word was always gold. You could trust what he said to you. It was a privilege to call both men my friends. The strength of the relationships that Jon Hanson and I had with Well Mara and his son John, Leon Hess, and Steve Gutman, the president of the Jets, enabled us to accomplish things that were truly unique and innovative. For example, we built additional stadium suites and restaurant areas as an equal three-way partnership that benefitted all parties.

Other relationships forged along the way included one with Tom Jernstedt, vice president of the NCAA and manager of the Division I Men's Basketball Tournament. Next was Bill Hancock, who was the onsite director for all the NCAA basketball programs. Bill subsequently ran the Bowl Championship Series (BCS) game for the Athletic Directors Association and is now the executive director of the College Football Championship and the National Championship Game.

Like many other aspects in life, relationships are critically important to our successes and reputations because they help us achieve our goals.

Some anecdotes among many that speak to the importance of relationships include a July 4 holiday in 1989 on Nantucket Island. In the spring of that year, I was trying to get Notre Dame to play in the upcoming Kickoff Classic. The legendary Lou Holtz, then the coach of the Fighting Irish, turned down the NJSEA's first three suggestions of opponents for various reasons. One of his objections was that he didn't want to set up a defensive game plan to face a one-back offense he would never see during the regular season. So I had to find an opponent that Notre Dame would agree to play.

This is where my prior relationship with George Welsh, previously a coach at Navy and now the head coach of Virginia, enabled me to talk directly to him about playing Notre Dame. George was trying to recruit running back Terry Kirby, who became one of Virginia's all-time greats, and thus the Cavaliers agreed to play Notre Dame that fall because it would help with recruiting Kirby.

Part of the Kickoff Classic's far-reaching impact was the creation of relationships with the corporate community of New Jersey. This particular year, Ed Hennessey, then the chairman and CEO of Allied Signal, was the Kickoff Classic's corporate chairman. He would be vacationing on his yacht over the July 4 holiday in Nantucket and suggested that we join him to celebrate the finalization of the matchup.

George Welsh invited us to stay at his home on the island, and Father Edmund Joyce, the renowned vice president of Notre Dame, was a guest. We all had dinner on the evening of July 3 in the dining room of the yacht, and on Independence Day, we celebrated the arrangement of the game with a champagne-and-eggs breakfast on the beach at the tip of Nantucket Island. It was a relaxed and happy time.

On a business note, while attempting to shore up the image of the Meadowlands during the telecast of the 1996 Final Four, I hosted a dinner in New York at the 21 Club for CBS Sports personnel. On-air announcers Jim Nantz and Billy Packer were among the attendees. Also there were members of the NCAA Men's Basketball Tournament staff, including Tom Jernstedt and Bill Hancock. Some from my staff, along with former Seton Hall coach and legendary announcer Billy Raftery, who was on retainer for us, were present.

The purpose of the dinner was to make sure that CBS understood that I did not want to hear comments like "Here in the shadows of New York" or that this was a "New York City Final Four" broadcasted over the airwaves. This Final Four was New Jersey's, and the nation and world needed to know that. Needless to say, I accomplished my objective.

Later, during my time as the AD at Rutgers, I received a call from entrepreneur and future president Donald Trump. He called to ask if he could film an episode of his successful network television show *The Apprentice* during an upcoming Rutgers home football game against Navy. To prepare for filming at the game, Trump and members of his production staff flew to Rutgers via helicopter (landing on one of the practice fields on the Busch Campus) one morning to scout out locations and get some background footage for the show. We had the Rutgers Marching Band and cheerleaders on hand at 7:30 in the morning to give them the opportunity to obtain some authentic footage.

But strong relationships aren't always reserved for power brokers or deal makers. I've always found it necessary to build trusting connections across the board, and at Rutgers, that meant with alumni, administrators, and staff from throughout the university as well as with the parents of our student athletes.

In one instance, after a controversial and emotionally draining loss in one of our sports, I got a call from the NCAA office in Indianapolis. They told me that after the game, they had received a terroristic call threatening their headquarters. The NCAA traced the call and wanted me to know that it came from the parents of one of the players on the team. I told them that in all likelihood, it was just a knee-jerk reaction and an emotional response to the loss. I contacted the parents and suggested they get a lawyer and then apologize immediately for making the call to the NCAA, which they did, and the issue ended.

You never know where tough and controversial losses could end up. It shows you in today's world where emotional situations might lead. In addition, you never know where the everyday life of an AD will take you.

My service on the board of the NFF and College Football Hall of Fame for 21 years, including 15 years as the chairman of the Awards Committee, led to the establishment of a number of relationships that have proved beneficial through the years. It began with the Kickoff Classic and Bob Casciola, the former head coach at Connecticut and Princeton who later became the executive director and chief operating officer of the NFF.

My time on the NFF board was very fruitful. Great friendships developed with folks like Joe Castiglione, the AD at Oklahoma; Steve Hatchell, the former commissioner of the Big 8 who is now president of the NFF; Chris Plonsky, the highly respected women's AD at Texas; Clay Bennett, chairman of the ownership group of the NBA's Oklahoma City Thunder; Bob Bowlsby, commissioner of the Big 12 and former AD at Stanford; and Mike Slive, commissioner of the Southeastern Conference (SEC).

Other members of the board included former Dallas Cowboys quarterback Troy Aikman; David Davis of the Rose Bowl; Jeffrey Immelt, then chairman and CEO of General Electric; NFL owners Jerry Jones (Dallas Cowboys) and Bob Kraft (New England Patriots); and the late business magnate and philanthropist T. Boone Pickens.

These are all examples, among many, of how strong and long-term relationships help achieve significant outcomes. Those partnerships certainly enabled me to accomplish many other worthwhile goals throughout my career.

These were among the formative experiences I drew on in my life and my career as I prepared to lead Rutgers University athletics from almost nonexistence to national prominence. St. Augustine wrote, "The degree to which you are concerned for the common good rather than your own can judge how much progress you have made." It's a guide I have never forgotten.

CHAPTER 3

LONG OVERDUE
FOR CHANGE

At a press conference on April 15, 1998, the president of Rutgers University, Dr. Francis L. Lawrence—Fran, as he warmly invited his friends to call him—introduced me as the college's new AD.

The audience included people I knew well, some who knew of me, and others who either supported or scorned intercollegiate sports and Rutgers's place in national college athletics.

I intended my opening words, written the night before, to announce a vision for the program. A vision that was believable, achievable, inclusive, and farsighted. Neither pie in the sky nor unexciting but somewhere in between, offering a goal of reaching greatness.

I told Fran and the others in the room that there are many universities where academics, cultural activities, intramural recreation, and Division I athletics combine to create an extraordinarily rich, diverse campus life. For decades, Rutgers had steadily and impressively moved toward the upper levels of that distinguished list. My goal was for the program to help the university earn the top position.

I spoke about the welfare of student athletes. I also spent time with the two student athletes who were part of the Search Committee. Some might have thought, *They're only students. Shouldn't he be forming elite ties, glad-handing with senior university officials, faculty, donors, and alumni? Aren't they his most important constituents on his first day of work?*

They would have been mistaken. I wanted to listen to the two student athletes' views because they were my most important constituents. Without them, there was no athletic department or programs.

Our focus had to be on the student athletes: their individual visions to achieve excellence on the athletic stage and across their total college experience. It's unfortunate that today, too many institutions are only interested in winning. The athlete is an instrument in what began as a traditionally noble endeavor but more often resembles a corrupted venture. ADs and their staffs have a responsibility to each and every student playing Division I sports to prepare him or her for life academically first, athletically second, and as forthcoming members of American and global society third.

I arrived at Rutgers ready to ask practical questions: What's already in place? Has it made Rutgers a better university and our student athletes finer young men and women? When was the last time anyone independently reviewed the current athletic programs as succeeding or falling short? Is this the best we can do?

And most important, we asked ourselves, "Where do we begin?" During my tenure as the Rutgers AD, I was sincere in referring to myself and our team—the assistant ADs, administrative staff, coaches, and support personnel—as *we*. Each individual was dedicated to our program's sport-specific and strategic missions. We understood that our efforts should represent a record of accomplishments greater than any single person's contribution. We always operated as one team of professionals committed to Rutgers's success on and off the field.

In our first six months at Rutgers, my staff spotted several areas that needed attention—some sooner than later, but all of them equally important. Each was vital to rebuilding and, in some instances, transforming the organization.

I had a core team of five in the beginning: Joe Quinlan, the new Senior Associate AD; Kevin MacConnell, Associate AD; John Wooding, Sports Information Director; Linda Markowitz, my executive assistant; and

Kathleen Conlin, Kevin's executive assistant. All were central to what we accomplished at Rutgers. Their competence and loyalty to our mission were exceptional.

My style of leadership was to bring one essential person with me from my previous position. It would be someone who represented competence, loyalty, and strong interpersonal skills. This individual also had to know the business and how I wanted things done.

When I went to the State Department of Corrections, that person was Jim Stabile, a local newspaper editor. Judith Nallin-DiGiandomenico, a brilliant lawyer who worked with me on prison issues in the governor's counsel office, also joined me at corrections as the deputy commissioner. When I went to the NJSEA, it was Michael Rowe from the governor's office. And when I went to Rutgers, I brought Joe Quinlan. Joe had been an assistant AD at both Seton Hall and St. Bonaventure universities before becoming the assistant director of the NCAA Division I Men's Basketball Tournament. I recruited him to the NJSEA to work on our Final Four team. He served as the Senior Associate AD and Deputy AD for me at Rutgers and later went on to become the AD at both Seton Hall and Saint Peter's. He is now the Associate AD at Columbia.

As for others who already worked at their posts when I arrived, I encouraged and welcomed them to show their depth of knowledge and abilities for the work we did.

I believe everyone deserves an equal opportunity; I do not agree that wholesale firings and "cleaning house" are effective ways to show strong leadership. My approach at Rutgers also provided an important asset to the staff. I wanted them to know they could go to someone in management and discuss issues without feeling at risk. Joe Quinlan was a superb conduit in his role. If Joe could solve the problem, he did. If he knew he had to bring it to me, he would.

I've also been fortunate to have assistants in my life who were very competent and loyal and had their "ears to the ground" to keep me apprised of ongoing and important issues. These valuable staffers were Marie Gervasio while I was in government in Trenton, Carol Baron during my 19-year tenure at the NJSEA, and Linda Markowitz during my 11 years at Rutgers. They were terrific and became part of our family. Incidentally, two of them were already employed at their respective positions when I arrived, and all three were able to establish outstanding working relationships with me.

At Rutgers, our first challenge was to change the athletic department's culture. Its people were loyal, and we respected their views about all aspects of the general program. This was a dedicated team of professionals—coaches, assistants, and support staff. They possessed a genuine work ethic that impressed me.

At the same time, their morale was low, and I understood why. The athletics program suffered from too many years of lackluster win-loss records. It was a culture that been beaten down—one that came to accept mediocrity—and that had to change. The program also lacked sufficient money and resources for its size and the national profile we wanted to achieve. Yet I knew it was not the staff simply being comfortable with a "status quo" state of mind. Being underpaid and overworked worsened an already poor morale.

The Olympic sports coaches (on the Division I level, programs other than football and basketball are referred to as "Olympic" sports) in particular suffered from insufficient resources. The programs weren't just lacking dollars; the coaches felt like abandoned children with no emotional support, as one of them told me. "We were fragmented by a 'divide and conquer' mentality from within," another coach said.

By the way, not all the coaches necessarily understood or were ready to accept that new leadership could positively affect their coaching methods, team goals, and player attitudes. The challenge for coaches who preceded my arrival as the AD was that they had forgotten what it felt like to see daylight. Generally speaking, they had grown discouraged with a system that had operated the same way—namely, too much resistance to change—with often disappointing results for 25 years. But my team and I did not believe that anyone thought it was OK to continue being average. The coaches seemed ready for improvements across the board. Fans, donors, students, student athletes, and athletics staff understood that some long-awaited changes were inevitable.

Everyone was impatient for more wins, fewer losses, division and conference titles, postseason bowl and tournament invitations, and long-awaited positive publicity. Aware that it would take time, the Rutgers personnel listened and were willing to support the principal objectives I wanted us to attain.

I was determined to reach those goals as one team, and I told them as much. Together we would

- raise student athlete academic performance and graduation rates;
- improve and expand team practice, training, and game-day facilities;
- elevate the perception of Rutgers athletics across the university, in New Jersey, within the NCAA and other sport-specific conferences, and on the national stage; and
- post winning records, attain championship titles, and set records in team and student athlete achievements in every sport.

Our second challenge was the athletics leadership's location and access. My predecessor's office was on College Avenue on New Brunswick's main campus in the old gymnasium, lovingly called "the Barn." That building had a lot of history attached to it, particularly the NCAA men's basketball team's run to the Final Four in 1976. AD Fred Gruninger, along with other administrators and some coaching staff, had worked out of that facility for decades.

But the majority of Fred's organization and staff worked at the Rutgers Athletic Center (RAC) on the Livingston Campus, across the Raritan River in Piscataway. Fred remained headquartered in the Barn, thinking it mattered, I believe, for the AD to be in New Brunswick—close to the president's office at Old Queens. And office space at the RAC was sorely lacking.

I understood Fred's views, but I had a different opinion. Rutgers's athletics programs needed and deserved to be together in order to work as a
team—to feel like a community with easy access to each other.

I firmly believe a leader should be available and highly visible. At Rutgers, I even placed my desk in an open area on the mezzanine above the
basketball floor. Things stayed that way until we raised sufficient funds to
build enclosed offices.

Setting up our new base of operations extended a message for the
future: we would work as a team to raise the level of athletics competition
at Rutgers. It helped coming to Rutgers before computers, smartphones,
and mobile devices made text and email messages the most convenient
forms of communicating and doing business. It meant that people had to
address each other in person.

The challenges Rutgers athletics faced required direct conversations.
We would solve them through understanding, listening, planning, and
executing a revitalized strategy and development plan. In today's tech-
based world, working face-to-face with others still matters. I regret that it
is overlooked too often, only utilized as a second choice, and sometimes
deemed simply unnecessary.

I remember the conversations Joe Quinlan and I had in those early
months. He told me about the line of people outside his cubicle every
day—one person needed this, another person needed help with that. Joe
admitted that he started questioning what he signed up for by coming
with me to Rutgers. Yet each night on his long drive home, he was excited
as he thought about our mission to build a tremendous program.

Getting staff into new offices was urgent. That meant we needed money.
I thought someone was pulling my leg when I found out the department's
annual budget for capital improvements was a paltry $125,000—nowhere
near enough to provide and maintain the facilities we needed to be competitive. But it wasn't someone's idea of a joke; raising funds to reconstruct and
support an athletics program in the years ahead would be a major priority.

Bob guest lecturing at Marian Rosenwasser's Rutgers graduate leadership class, 2017. Marian is the former women's head tennis coach and is a widely respected leader in the athletic department.

Everyone who stood with me and shared my vision understood that this was exactly how change happened. We wanted each member and every group in the new athletics organization to succeed. They wanted exactly the same thing. We had an opportunity to help them perform and achieve at a level they previously only imagined reaching. This wouldn't happen in a day or even a year, but it definitely was going to happen. I promised them.

The third challenge was to change the way different constituents—from student athletes, faculty, and alumni to the people of New Jersey—perceived Rutgers. The program had operated for too long without clear goals. The department didn't know what it was like to share a unified purpose. They suffered, somewhat proudly, through decades of frustration and lost hope.

I was committed to change. I wanted everyone who respected and followed Rutgers to believe that its sports teams could and would win at the

Bob with longtime friend George Steinbrenner at Yankee Stadium, 1980s.

highest levels of intercollegiate sports in five years or less. I also found out that achieving those expectations would take time and would be difficult. It simply motivated and encouraged me more.

Fourth were the relationships that athletics had with President Francis Lawrence and his senior administration—specifically Joe Whiteside, Senior Vice President and Treasurer; the Rutgers Boards of Governors, Trustees, and Overseers; and the Rutgers University Foundation with Brian Crockett. Brian was very helpful, making sure I knew the key alumni and getting me in front of them. He had a deep love for the university that harkened back to his days as a letter winner for Rutgers football.

Fifth was rebuilding a unified direction, with all the resources my staff expected, so they and every aspect of Rutgers athletics could succeed. Terry Beachem, John Ternyila, and Natalie Migliaro from the athletics business office; Doug Kokoskie of facilities and operations; Rob Monaco, our team doctor and director of our sports medicine program; and many of the

Olympic sports coaches—including Marian Rosenwasser (tennis), Bob Reasso (soccer), and Maura Waters-Ballard (golf)—were leaders in helping us rebuild and change the culture. I relied on them for honest advice and historical knowledge, and they always gave it to me. Most of all, they wanted what was best for Rutgers. They had been there long enough to acknowledge that change was long overdue.

To say we had our work cut out for us is an understatement. Yet this was exactly the set of challenges I looked for when I passed up George Steinbrenner's offer to join the Yankees and chose to lead Rutgers athletics proudly and successfully on the national stage of Division I sports. Building a new program is sometimes easier than resurrecting a weakened one.

I knew the secret of leadership was having a vision, clearly communicating it to everyone, and then executing it. Most importantly, I had to take ownership of that vision. You cannot be a successful leader without taking responsibility for your program. It is the organizational culture you create that determines the success you can achieve. It is critically important for everyone to feel that they have a role to play and a place in your operation.

CHAPTER 4

REBUILDING A
PROGRAM

Today's ADs face a variety of complex and diverse issues. This chapter addresses many of the critical problems my department faced and illustrates how we solved these issues as they arose. The past can provide context for the present. What follows are examples of some major concerns that confronted us along the path to implementing our vision.

Compliance

Not all issues were unknown or unexpected when we started out. "Compliance" with NCAA rules and guidelines is one of the most important responsibilities for every intercollegiate athletic program in the country. For example, programs that do not meet basic eligibility requirements can find themselves out of business easily and quickly.

We didn't waste any time determining whether Rutgers's programs and its athletes were compliant with NCAA rules. I was appointed AD in February 1998 and actually took over later that year in April. During the transition period, the news my team and I received was not all bad—but just not exactly good. I had several meetings with Fred Gruninger, the outgoing AD, who was very forthright and helpful in the transition. I needed to know as much as possible about the program, and Fred was the best resource to provide this information. I asked Fred several questions: Do we have any violations now? Are we certain we don't or is it that we don't know of any? Who knows and who is responsible for Rutgers managing its compliance? If we have any violations, how many are there and what's our situation with each of them?

The answer I got from Fred was that we had a few minor violations. That was generally positive news, but it could be because there was just one compliance officer monitoring 30 programs and nearly 800 student athletes. In addition, the officer's job description included many other responsibilities besides compliance. That meant we had less than one full-time person working with compliance issues, a near-impossible task. Rightfully, it immediately became one of my biggest concerns.

Compliance can be a difficult business. Just ask Syracuse University and its men's basketball program, which found out about decade-long problems and violations when they became headline news in March 2015.

Still, there's no getting around it: there are rules for everything, including roster sizes and the hours and dates teams can practice and compete in a given week. There are also all kinds of regulations about recruiting: Which coaches are eligible to go on the road to recruit? What can a recruiter say and not say? When is it all right and when it is off-limits for a recruiter to speak to an athlete?

If a coach "ran into" a recruit during an off-campus event and said hello with people standing around, someone was bound to notice it—and maybe say something about it to someone else. Rumors spread and problems developed even when nothing inappropriate or impermissible took place. This was at a time before social media.

As an AD, I could occasionally invite a student athlete to my home for dinner if I lived within 50 miles of the university. Yet it was entirely different when my family was on vacation in New England, where the Cape Cod summer baseball league drew some of the top college prospects in the United States to play. If I saw one of our student athletes at a game and wanted to have him over for dinner, I was not allowed to offer an invitation in my role as an AD due to NCAA rules.

One of my first moves was asking officials at the Big East Conference office if they could recommend a top-notch compliance officer I could hire. We were in luck. They said that Kate Hickey, a respected associate at the Big East, might be interested. This was promising news. Kate was bright, she was well-liked by coaches and officials across the conference, and most of all, she had a comprehensive understanding of intercollegiate athletics compliance matters—exactly what we needed immediately.

Kate accepted my invitation to meet and talk about our plans for rebuilding Rutgers athletics on the national level, focusing more effectively and fully on compliance, and the opportunity for her to play a major role in fulfilling our vision.

She was definitely interested but didn't accept my offer right away; she was considering other proposals. More important, Kate knew there had been compliance issues at Rutgers involving the incumbent compliance officer, which were complicated by an uneasy relationship with the previous AD. Many at the conference headquarters were aware of this too.

First, the two Rutgers officials did not trust each other. Second, there were too many programs and student athletes for a staff of just one compliance officer, working in the position half-time, to manage. Finally, no one could answer important questions about the athletic program's compliance record—its number of outstanding violations (if there were any) and how they were being resolved. These were among the questions I posed before arriving on campus.

Kate eventually agreed to join my staff, and I was enormously pleased. We were fortunate to get her. She did terrific work for our programs and our athletes, and especially for Rutgers University overall, and continues to do so. I learned to rely on Kate's keen judgment and dependable advice as she quickly became one of my most trusted advisors. She also joined many NCAA committees and was respected enough to chair the NCAA's Management Council and the council's Legislative Review Subcommittee.

After she studied our circumstances, Kate came to us. "We should be concerned about eligibility," she said.

A routine compliance review revealed that the system we inherited at Rutgers was deeply flawed. It suffered from internal miscommunications and false assumptions involving different university staffs simultaneously monitoring compliance. The checks and balances did not work fully or effectively.

Rutgers was not guilty of flagrant eligibility violations—not the kinds that result in newspaper headlines, anyway—but that didn't matter now. We reworked our strategies and plans to be fully compliant and eligible for every program. I wanted to ensure Kate had additional confirmation for any issues she uncovered and our recommendations for settling them.

I went to see Rutgers president Fran Lawrence. "Our new compliance officer informed me we may have some potential problems with compliance and eligibility going on," I said.

Wanting Kate to have my backing on this, I also asked for President Lawrence's support to hire a consultant to investigate Kate's concerns. We had to corroborate the problems and their extent. "Definitely," he said. "Go ahead."

We hired Dale Smith, a consultant with experience in compliance issues. His instructions were to audit the program. Several weeks later, both Kate and Dale came to see me. Dale confirmed the things that had concerned Kate. We had a problem but did not know its extent.

I went back to see President Lawrence—he always invited me to call him Fran, which I sincerely appreciated—and this time I asked for permission to retain the legal services of Bond, Schoeneck & King and one of its lead attorneys, Richard Evrard. I specifically wanted Richard because of his prior experience with the NCAA. Bond, Schoeneck & King is a nationally respected Kansas City–based law firm that specializes in intercollegiate sports compliance matters. Again, President Lawrence accepted my recommendation. I was grateful for Fran's strong support, especially in my initial months as the director of the athletic program.

We spent the next year going through the files of an estimated 2,000 student athletes, checking the eligibility of each one. The results were discouraging because although the mistakes were not ones of commission, there were numerous errors of omission.

Managing intercollegiate sports compliance and eligibility so student athletes can play and graduate successfully is a difficult process.

Joe Quinlan contacted Tom Yeager, the commissioner of the Colonial Athletic Association and a respected individual in NCAA sports leadership (he served as the chairman of the Infractions Committee). We spoke with him and explained our process, its problems, and my pledge as the new AD to put any eligibility infractions behind us as soon as possible.

It was a good first step. Tom suggested we create a "self-report" in which we would state any violations and propose self-imposed penalties. That way, we could prove to NCAA officials that we were serious about resolving any outstanding violations. The Infractions Committee would then review our recommendations, and they could either add to or lessen our self-imposed penalties or launch their own investigation.

For instance, we had options with scholarships. Football, men's and women's basketball, and soccer had specific caps on the number of scholarships we could award. The Olympic sports (e.g., swimming, diving, wrestling, and gymnastics) required a different calculation because their limits were equivalent; thus you could award partial aid to student athletes, limited by the dollar amount of the total number of scholarships awarded.

Producing an honest, self-prepared report was a difficult process. It meant we would be making tough decisions about penalties we would impose on our student athletes. However, choosing this method also meant that the NCAA could accept our recommendations and decide not to perform its own independent investigation.

After reviewing all the facts carefully with our staff and lawyers, we decided to self-report and put ourselves on probation for two years. We also cut 20 scholarships from sports that had eligibility problems.

I offer one situation as an example. The student was a football player entering his senior year with one year of eligibility left. Problems developed when we discovered that an academic advisor had unwittingly enrolled him in a noneligible three-credit course his junior year. Because of that inadvertent error, he had neither the requisite credits to play his senior year nor the time left to correct the issue. Furthermore, he had competed for a season while he was not eligible to do anything—practice, train, or suit up on game day.

The NCAA's position is clear: student athletes are responsible for their own course selections and their eligibility. But it was events like the example with the football player—a lack of knowledge of NCAA rules and a lack of proper oversight in the department—that put us in our situation to begin with.

It was tough telling the player's family that because their son received bad academic advice, he was ineligible to play football his senior year. It was especially difficult because some NFL scouts considered him a prospect, and he obviously would have benefitted from additional practice, training, and playing time in games. In numerous other cases, the violations were primarily clerical errors and missing paperwork—yet they were still violations. Collectively, they added up.

The incident with the football player is also a glaring example of the pitfalls that universities can encounter when they do not provide proper resources and funding to run their athletic departments correctly.

I thought what we did at Rutgers was fair. It also showed confidence on our part. I wanted to present a position on compliance that met conditions forthright going in and let the NCAA see it as an appropriate response.

And they did. I wanted to establish credibility with Tom Yeager because I was the new AD and was determined for Rutgers to move forward. I firmly believed we were better off showing them that we could take care of our own problems.

It was the right decision. The NCAA accepted our report with a couple of minor revisions and said they were not going to investigate.

Over time, Kate built a staff that oversaw all teams and continuously worked to make sure coaches and staff knew their responsibilities. It has paid off in spades and continues to do so. Centralizing responsibility for all sports required all my coaches to meet their primary duties.

Cutting Sports Programs

The most contentious issue we faced during my years at Rutgers was the decision to cut some intercollegiate sports programs. It drew a lot of criticism, which I anticipated. Whether someone agreed or disagreed with eliminating any programs, the bottom line was that it was a university-based financial decision.

When I became the AD, President Lawrence showed me two studies. One was an internal review of the athletic program conducted by the trustees and chaired by Ron Giaconia. The other was an external review from a group led by Gene Corrigan, a former NCAA president, AD at both Virginia and Notre Dame, and commissioner of the Atlantic Coast Conference (ACC). Both studies concluded that Rutgers had more sports programs than it could adequately fund. In reality, the reports revealed what we already knew: we needed more money or fewer sports.

It was also much more complicated than dollars in or programs out. We were dealing with a nearly unwinnable situation that had started decades earlier. When I came in, few of the Olympic sports head coaches worked full time. There were few assistant coaches throughout the programs, and some were only earning $7,000 to $8,000 annually without benefits. We built a salary plan that got them up to $12,500, then $25,000 with benefits.

Being a land-grant institution that became a state school in the 1950s, Rutgers operated for decades with tight restrictions on its budgets. It depended mostly on appropriations approved by the state legislature and little else. Until the 1990s, Rutgers lacked a historical record for raising money from alumni and other sources to establish endowments, support athletics, open new academic disciplines, and finance large-scale capital improvements. The university was simply cash poor without being in the poorhouse.

Rutgers also never benefited from longtime political or alumni support—the kind that allowed state universities such as Penn State, Michigan, Texas, and Iowa to flourish and grow in academics, build a global presence, maintain and expand infrastructure, and compete at the top tiers of national intercollegiate athletics. While it is the State University of New Jersey, Rutgers is relatively young in that role compared to the schools it competes with. Rutgers did not become the state university until 1956.

Those limitations have negatively affected Rutgers's standing. Moreover, financing sports has also been a longtime struggle at Rutgers. The university community and the Board of Governors were always concerned, sometimes to an unreasonable degree, about spending money on athletics.

There is much truth to the idea that you must invest in something if you want it to succeed. Specifically, Rutgers could not compete at a high level without giving their coaches and student athletes the resources they needed. That did not mean excessive spending, but it did mean building and maintaining first-class facilities.

The state budget crisis of 2006 forced Rutgers to make dramatic cuts throughout the university. The university implored members of the community, including its vast New Jersey alumni base, to appeal to their state legislators to restore proposed cuts to the budget. "Help Keep Rutgers Strong for New Jersey" read one of the campaign's pieces, adding that the proposed budget would leave Rutgers with an estimated $114 million shortfall: "The university is looking at cost-saving measures, but a cut of this size would force a large increase in tuition, the cancellation of hundreds of classes and reductions in the very research and outreach activities that drive New Jersey's economic growth."[1]

Al Gamper, chairman of the Board of Governors, wanted cuts in everything from "athletics to zoology." Therefore, the athletic department was not exempt from those cuts.

I still had to decide what our priorities should and would be for athletics. My duty was to present a budget proposal that would be both fair and realistic given what we had to work with—not nearly enough money.

When the university decided to follow the course of big-time athletics in the early 1970s, the schedules may have changed, but proper funding lagged far behind. Because of this, Rutgers has been forced to play catch-up throughout its journey at this level.

I started by asking the New Jersey State Interscholastic Athletic Association (NJSIAA) to tell us the number of high school athletes competing in sports programs across the state. I thought the information could provide a baseline to help us when making cuts and awarding assistance.

Unfortunately, we did not gain any headway or make much progress. We already fielded teams representing the top 19 programs participating under the NJSIAA's supervision.

During my years at the NJSEA and specifically during my time at Rutgers, I worked with the NJSIAA to hold high school tournament and championship games on campus. I wanted to establish a strong relationship between Rutgers and secondary school programs for the future.

Meanwhile, we had to deal with another concern tied to altering the menu of programs we offered. It was Title IX, the ban on discrimination based on sex at educational institutions that accepted federal funds and became law in 1972.

While the original federal statute did not explicitly state gender equity and equal opportunity in athletics, that's exactly how Americans have always viewed Title IX. Moreover, the programs that were at risk of being cut or losing their varsity status could have also included women's teams.

This was a difficult process for me and all team staffs. Being long on hope but short on cash, we could no longer sustain every sports team at the varsity level.

The Board of Governors did not want to deal with this issue because it was a sensitive subject, and many people had personal feelings about it. Twice in earlier years, I had submitted recommendations for resizing the athletic program to the Athletic Committee, chaired by Ron Giaconia. After the discussions ended, Ron and the committee members told me to remove all papers relating to the issue. It was that sensitive.

Originally, there were options to cut more sports, but they were unten-
able. Aware that any cuts would draw criticism, our final recommendations changed all three levels of men's varsity rowing—heavyweight,
lightweight, and freshmen—to club sports. Our rationale was that as a
club sport, men's crew teams could compete in all the regattas already on
their schedule, with the exception of the Intercollegiate Rowing Association (IRA) Championships, traditionally called the IRAs by rowers in the
United States. We also cut men's swimming and diving, men's tennis, and
men's and women's fencing but didn't touch any other women's teams to
stay within the guidelines for Title IX.

The process of reaching a final recommendation came from an internal athletic department committee composed of both staff and coaches. I
accepted their conclusions and delivered them to the president.

The Board of Governors wanted the cuts implemented immediately. At
its meeting in May 2006, I spoke up. While we really did not have a choice,
I thought it was unethical to cut programs on such short notice. The student athletes affected wouldn't have enough time to transfer to schools
where they could compete again for the upcoming season. Even though
we would hold off for one more year, we also intended to announce the
actions the board approved and agreed we could carry them out.

I urged giving the affected students time to transfer if they wanted to,
affording them better odds of competing as varsity athletes in their sports
at different universities. I also believed being transparent about this issue
was critical.

I was adamant on these points, and the board agreed. We also agreed
that students on scholarship would maintain their scholarships as long as
they stayed in school. No coaches suffered salary cuts. They were already
underpaid, and I tried to work it out so no coach took a financial hit.

The criticism was unrelenting, particularly from the crew community
and a lone parent from the fencing community. They constantly requested
department records under the state's Open Public Records Act, which
we always complied with. Most important is to understand that I did

not make those decisions unilaterally. I presented my views to President Richard McCormick and the Board of Governors, and they supported my recommendations. They were fully informed, had vetted the recommendations, and gave their full support—with one exception.

George Zoffinger, a member of the Board of Governors, was a constant antagonist toward our program goals and particularly toward my leadership. One time he offered to resign his seat if I agreed to reinstate the six programs we cut from intercollegiate competition. More important, he was unwilling to meet with us to listen to our positions and to express his own so we could understand them too. He preferred being a repeated opponent toward anything and everything we set out to achieve for Rutgers athletics—and Rutgers University.

As time has borne out, making this decision, although a very difficult one, has proven to be the right one. The difficulty in funding 24 sports, let alone 30, has demonstrated the necessity of this action. The athletic department's financial filing with the NCAA for the 2014–2015 season showed that Rutgers football turned a profit of just over $8 million, while men's basketball was approximately $900,000 in the black.

Rutgers's 22 other sports, all with the support provided by student fees and institutional subsidies, still lost, from a low $274,000 (men's golf) to a high of $2.6 million (women's basketball). The original intent of the student fees was to provide support for the Olympic sports and also enable the overall student body to enjoy the experience of intercollegiate athletic events at no additional cost.

Budget and Finance

Responsibility and accountability have always been priorities throughout the various stops in my career. At Rutgers, these tenets transcended all areas of our operations, including academics, the welfare and well-being of our student athletes, coaching, budgetary and financial matters, and facilities and operations.

Our financial processes came under undue scrutiny during the latter portion of my tenure at Rutgers. Headlines screamed of "off-the-books spending" and "secret contracts"—perhaps these incendiary bylines were attempts to sell newspapers in an era of falling circulation.

There was just no way any of those allegations could be true. All our finances and spending were accounted for in budgets and contracts, with the complete knowledge of the Rutgers administration. In addition, our chief financial officer Terry Beachem developed a detailed process to establish our budget, which culminated in the administration signing off on it at the end of each fiscal year.

There's an old adage that goes, "You need to spend money to make money." Unfortunately, this was a rather novel concept at Rutgers, despite the many challenges we faced in building the athletics program. As our program grew in stature, we felt we needed to invest and reinvest to continue our momentum.

The bottom line is that Rutgers committed to competing at a high level decades ago, and in order to do so, inadequate facilities and coaching contracts that were simply not representative of the marketplace had to be addressed.

For example, there was much criticism of Greg Schiano's contract and salary as the football program reached new heights. Put simply, Rutgers—and to a larger degree, New Jersey—was not used to having a successful program. Greg was the consensus national coach of the year following our memorable 2006 campaign, when we finished ranked number 12 in the country with an 11–2 record. He deserved to be compensated at a competitive rate—and comparatively speaking, it was not outlandish.

There are only about 120 Division I college football coaches in the world, and Greg had ascended to the upper tier. Think about this: he built a program that had been winless a decade earlier and was regularly the butt of national jokes.

But New Jersey wasn't ready for its state university's college football coach to be the highest-paid state employee. Are things skewed when it comes to the salaries of athletes and coaches in our world of sports? Maybe, but that's the reality that we presently live in. In addition to his student athletes' success on the field, in the classroom, and in the community, Greg was also instrumental in helping position Rutgers for its eventual entrance into the Big Ten (B1G) Conference—certainly the upper echelon of college academics and athletics combined. The improvements we made in areas such as academics and facilities went a long way to showing our commitment to becoming a part of that esteemed grouping.

We needed to bring Rutgers Stadium up to speed. It was a must if we were to continue our ascension. Closing in the south end zone to provide an additional 11,000 seats and adding a club level were necessary enhancements. Other improvements included an updated scoreboard that was representative of a first-class program and putting in field turf to allow for year-round use. We also ensured that the foundations were in place for a future expansion of the stadium.

In a conversation with me, Terry Beachem recalled a shift in the financial process in 2002:

> During my 27-year tenure as Chief Financial Officer, I instituted an annual budget planning and review process which typically would begin early in the spring semester and continue for several months until the operating budget was finalized for the fiscal year that began each July 1. This process would involve intense monitoring of the current year budget as well as preparing and refining several drafts of the ensuing year budget until we had balanced each year within or close to the authorized university subsidies. The budget process would typically involve several budget meetings with the Athletic Director and senior staff of the athletic department. As the status of the current year's operating budget was discussed, any known revenue shortfalls from football and basketball ticket sales were identified, explained and discussed.
>
> Another financial consequence resulting from football's competitive success was the fact that our head coach, Greg Schiano, became a highly

attractive candidate who was wooed by other universities with major
football programs, and in particular Miami. Greg had received an offer
from Miami and in order to keep Greg at Rutgers, Bob Mulcahy had to
present a counter offer to Greg's agent quickly. Part of Bob's counter offer
included new underwriting of a portion of Greg's new salary package
from new corporate sponsor revenues in the amount of $250,000. This
was *publicly disclosed* at the announcement of Coach Schiano's decision
to remain at Rutgers. Arranging for its implementation involved a consulting services contract between Schiano and Nelligan Sports Marketing (NSM) under which NSM would make the payment and account
for it in its annual financial settlement with Rutgers.

Various news media have alleged over the years that this deal on
behalf of Schiano amounted to "off the books spending" or "out of control spending by Rutgers." The allegations further accused the University
of intentionally hiding portions of Schiano's compensation package.
What the media failed to understand, or chose not to understand, is
that these costs were recorded on the University's books at the time that
the annual Nelligan financial settlement was received and recorded during the month of June. The additional $250,000 compensation arrange-
ment was reviewed and recorded in University accounts in entries made
by the University Controller after his review of the contract between
Schiano and NSM.[2]

The process we described simply would not allow for any irresponsible
spending, as the sensationalist-minded media claimed.

Finally, Terry explained how the university monitored our budget and
finances on a yearly basis: "Further, our annual financial reports were
reviewed and audited each year by Deloitte & Touche, the University's
independent auditors, under audit guidelines and procedures required by
the NCAA. NO AUDIT EXCEPTIONS were ever identified by the independent auditors in their annual audit reports."[3]

Constructing New Facilities

If Rutgers expected to be competitive in Division I and in the Big East Conference, it first needed student athletes and coaches who could win games and championships. In return, they required first-rate facilities worthy of the competition on their schedules.

When I showed up, Rutgers was much further ahead on talented athletes than athletic facilities. Both absolutely had to continue to improve quickly, especially our training sites and stadiums.

We estimated it would cost approximately $20 million to significantly restore, upgrade, and build new and modern facilities, including the Hale Center, team meeting rooms, football and basketball weight rooms, academic support program offices, and the Olympic sport teams' offices.

The academic support program's offices were converted concession stands off a concourse in the football stadium behind the football team's primary meeting room. The only way to get to them was to walk through the one existing football team meeting room.

Together, my staff, with significant input from head football coach Greg Schiano, created an ambitious plan. Between grants from the legislature and key individuals who were excited about the program's prospects and future, we raised $26 million. That valuable financial aid enabled us to accomplish many goals on our capital improvements list:

- enlarge the Hale Center
- upgrade and modernize the weight and training rooms, locker rooms, bleachers, and all team meeting and administrative offices
- paint the stadium red
- install synthetic turf in the football stadium and the baseball field
- provide the field hockey program with a new playing surface

Brian Crockett and later Jason Kroll, who worked with athletics through the Rutgers University Foundation, played major roles in our fund-raising efforts. Both were instrumental in our success.

Before our renovations, the baseball team practiced in an adjacent parking lot to the RAC anytime rain or snow turned the natural grass into a field of mud and water. Players would catch fly balls before they broke windshields and dented parked cars. This was not anyone's idea of a field of dreams.

Rutgers also had a sometimes good, sometimes not-so-good relationship with the state government in Trenton, particularly when it came to receiving financial support as a public university. The good part was that we were able to request and obtain a $500,000 appropriation annually in the state's budget for athletic capital projects, which was more than three times the capital budget when we first arrived. Thanks to my relationships with three New Jersey treasurers—David Rousseau, Brian Clymer, and John McCormac—this $500,000 arrangement remained in place until I was fired.

The bad part about Rutgers's dealings with state legislators and the governor's office was that they lacked relationships that were built on mutual trust and respect. Before I became the AD, the university did not have positive interactions with influential people in state government or the statehouse. Moreover, the governor's staff did not particularly have good rapport with Dick McCormick, who became president four years into my tenure as AD.

However, my personal relations with Senator Dick Codey (D) and Senator John Bennett (R) paid off with special appropriations during this period, with help from several key legislators. They included Senators Ray Lesniak (D) and Bob Littell (R), Assemblyman Walter Cavanaugh (R), and several others.

While financial and capital improvements challenges were large, I sincerely appreciated the outstanding support that our plans and projects and my leadership received from four senior university administrators. They were the late Joseph Whiteside, Senior Vice President and Treasurer; Nancy Winterbauer, Vice President of University Budgeting; Bruce Fehn, Senior Vice President for Finance and Administration; and Joanne Jackson, Senior Vice President and Treasurer who succeeded Joe Whiteside when he retired in 2000.

Joe, Nancy, Joanne, and Bruce always gave Rutgers athletics—and me personally—their interest and attention, their willingness to listen, and their genuine support during the internal battles for money that all universities inevitably experience.

They always expected my team to demonstrate how and why our requests for capital improvement appropriations should earn their approval. We did our best to prove it to them. They were professionals whom I respected and liked immensely. Most of all, they knew every major expenditure athletics made to improve the program and to enhance the experiences of our student athletes. Contrary to some media reports, every expenditure was accounted for either in the budget or in a contract.

Joe Whiteside worked very closely with my team and me. He played a major role in guiding our entry into the Big East as well as rebuilding Rutgers Stadium and the Hale Center into competitive, if not exceptional, facilities.

Since 2000 and Joe's passing, Rutgers has presented the Joseph P. Whiteside Award at convocation to a senior selected for exceptional academic ability and generous commitment to serving the community. I hope that all its recipients take time to understand the enormous service Joe Whiteside performed for Rutgers.

There were several alumni and supporters who were critical to helping us establish the foundation for future success. Kevin and Helen Collins, Gene and Lorna O'Hara, Mark and Charon Herschhorn, Ron and Toni Giaconia, Bill and Barbara Bauer, Felix and Doris Beck, Tom and Pat Werblin, Brian and Lois Perkins, Daniel Wheeler, Ron and Pat Bainton, Jerry and Lorraine Aresty, Steve Plofker and Bobbi Brown, Floyd and Helen Bragg, Dr. Peter and Elyse Jennings, Greg and Anna Brown, and John and Susan Herma were all influential supporters and donors. They were people I could rely on when I needed something.

Our efforts had a positive impact on the university. A prime example of this is the story of prominent alumnus Richard Shindell, a 1957 graduate and a former vice president at T. Rowe Price, and his wife, Donna. Jason Kroll recalled that the Shindells were donors to Rutgers but had the potential to significantly increase their contribution.

After initially meeting the Shindells, Jason learned about their genuine interests and set up a full day of on-campus meetings with them. Jason remembered that they were to meet with a variety of individuals, from athletics to recreation to neuroscience. After the Shindells spoke with Greg Schiano and then me, according to Jason, Richard said he had "never been prouder" of his alma mater.

The last meeting of the day was with Dr. Wise Young, one of—if not *the*—preeminent neuroscience researchers in the world. Wise was doing incredible research related to spinal cord injuries. Ultimately, Richard ended up making a gift totaling over $3 million to fund a professorship in neuroscience. He also made a $500,000 commitment in support of Rutgers football. He later became a member of the Rutgers University Foundation Board of Overseers.

No matter what the circumstances, my team tried to work with all divisions of the university, always hoping for a positive outcome for all involved, including athletics.

Stadium Expansion

Greg Schiano and the football team experienced great success in 2004, when they beat Michigan State in the season opener, and in 2005, with their first postseason appearance in 27 years at the Insight Bowl. Then on November 9, 2006, in the final two minutes of the Rutgers versus Louisville game at home, Rutgers won and made history. Thousands of students swarmed the field. Many loyal alumni and fans still call it the most dramatic moment and victory in Rutgers football history.

It certainly was. Close behind was our victory over Navy in October 2005, which made us bowl eligible. A memorable anecdote speaks to the wonderful relationship I had with the Rutgers marching band and with Tim Smith, its hardworking and committed director.

Hopefully anticipating victory against Navy and bowl eligibility on that late Saturday afternoon in October, I convinced Tim to let me lead the band with "When Irish Eyes Are Smiling" at the conclusion of the game. As I tried to conduct, I realized how difficult it was to lead the band, and my performance was incredibly poor. But the happiness of the moment more than made up for it. Rutgers would be going "bowling" for the first time since 1978! It was only the second time in its history and would mark the university's first national bowl appearance.

Those victories versus Navy in 2005 and Louisville and the football team's rising profile in the Big East reminded us that Rutgers Stadium needed more seats, period. Seismic shifts in conferences were beginning, with top-ranked schools entering and leaving. It was time for Rutgers and its football program to have a stadium with seating capacity and amenities that were on par with every other school in the Big East and in major college football. It would also prepare us for when we were considered for membership in another conference. We knew that without an enlarged and upgraded Rutgers Stadium, there would be no invitation to join the Big Ten Conference or any other major conference.

Perhaps it's true what they say: hindsight is 20/20. We can look back on hundreds of significant decisions we made during our lifetimes and question whether we would handle things differently if we had another chance.

That's how I reflect on our plans to enlarge the stadium. Many supported us. Some questioned whether the benefits would outweigh the costs, and I understood their concerns. A few antagonists were only satisfied when they criticized the plan.

I wanted my staff to focus on the long view, and I did my best to act just as I believed. We were already transforming Rutgers athletics from a regional contender to a competitor on the national stage. Reviews from alumni and students across the state and in the country were very encouraging.

As for agitators and malcontents with nothing better to do than disparage Rutgers's athletic future, I was not about to let them get in our way or hold us back. Our football success was earning national prestige and respect.

The football stadium's scoreboard was old and outdated and required immediate renovations. Making it right was essential, not a luxury or convenience, and upgrading it would cost an estimated $810,000. I asked several senior administrators at the university if they would be willing to loan athletics the money to do it, and they said no.

I called T. J. Nelligan, founder and owner of New Jersey–based Nelligan Sports Marketing. We retained them as our marketing partner in 2000 to improve the athletic program's marketing and visibility. T. J. was a smart businessman. He understood exactly what we needed, and our teams worked effectively together. Nelligan advanced the money for the scoreboard and was repaid annually by credits to our sponsorship dollars—a real example of working together. Nelligan's group also represented the Big East Conference and several of its member universities.

My main goal at Rutgers was to enact a broader strategy: Build a winning football program that received BCS ranking and significant bowl invitations. Sell out all the seats at every home game. Boost student and alumni support. Raise revenue to finance football operations independent of university appropriations. Above all, market and promote Rutgers athletics along with advancing the school's reputation for academic excellence as one of America's prestigious public research universities.

Creating capital-improvement projects and their budget estimates and then coming up with the money required is never easy, but I already had experience managing multimillion-dollar expansion projects due to my time at the NJSEA.

In addition, my experience as New Jersey's first Commissioner of Corrections—where I handled life-and-death situations—taught me resilience and patience to handle any difficulty I might encounter.

Rutgers presented different objections, sometimes confrontations. But these problems couldn't come close to producing the same level pressure I dealt with as commissioner of corrections and president of the NJSEA.

Yet some of my friends warned me that there were certain situations I might run into when doing business in a university culture. Oftentimes, objections and complaints could arise over petty or insignificant issues. Administrators would fight to protect their reputations and bases of power even when they knew it might stand in the way of the institution's best interests.

Unfortunately, academicians also tend to believe in processes that delay the opportunity to act. Universities are slow to change because "everything is a process," as they like to say. It's like turning an aircraft carrier around, which I had some experience doing as a naval officer.

I knew universities were not unique. Someone always feels determined to act against, rather than for, the good of an organization. It is human nature, and Rutgers was not an exception. Getting financial, political, and institutional support and approval to expand and improve the stadium was just another set of challenges to address. These were new names and faces, different agendas, and either practical questions or objections that usually wasted time and resources.

My team began serious conversations about expanding the stadium in 2004 despite the fact that we had won only 12 games over the previous four seasons. The 2004 season had been particularly frustrating because we opened with the big win over Michigan State on ABC TV and were 4–2 after six games. However, a car accident involving a drunk driver decimated our defensive backfield, seriously injuring two starters and a key reserve, which began the spiral to a 4–7 season.

Nonetheless, Greg Schiano and I hosted a meeting in the press box that December. We developed a vision for building a club level and suites, filling in the south end zone, and obtaining a new and modern scoreboard.

The New Brunswick Development Corporation (DEVCO), led by Chris Paladino, a prominent capital project builder and developer who has done so much to help his alma mater, financed a study to determine how well club seats, private suites, and end zone seats would sell. The response was good. When we were ready to start the project, the university wanted us to update the study, and the timing couldn't have been better. We organized a comprehensive study that included focus groups and interviews with season ticket holders and Rutgers alumni.

The responses were positive. They gave us ideas about pricing for suites and club seats as well as donations tied to both. In addition, the survey data helped us formulate ideas and preliminary plans to add an additional 12,000 seats. We retained HOK, a premier sports facility architecture firm from Kansas City.

Capital projects are often moving targets, which was also true with Rutgers. Our projected capital budget estimates were set and agreed to by the people and organizations involved. Then circumstances would change, and so did our budget estimates and agreements.

The original estimate was $120 million. The university said we could only develop a capital plan to spend $100 million. We decided to cut the suites because the club seats would pay for themselves quicker than the suites would. We ended up at a projected budget of $102 million.

In the early stages of our plans, we were encouraged that the state of New Jersey would subsidize the project with $30 million. The governor even sent his representative, Gary Rose, to a Finance Committee meeting of the Board of Governors to emphasize and ensure the state's commitment.

But then the state backed out after the governor's stem cell bond issue failed voter approval. Governor Corzine said he and state Senator Lesniak could raise $30 million.

Some at the statehouse in Trenton warned the governor that it would be unethical in his role as the state's chief executive officer to use his Rolodex of extensive contacts to raise the money. I found this out the night before the game against Louisville in 2007. It was going to be up to us in the athletic department and the university at large to come up with the $30 million that had been originally committed by the state.

In politics, it's not unusual for pledges to end up as promises unfulfilled. They excite, then disappoint. But this one hurt. The total raised by Governor Corzine and Senator Lesniak was $250,000, all from Governor Corzine personally. I knew all about expectations raised and fallen through from my time as the chief of staff to Governor Byrne, where I worked the corridors of the statehouse.

When the governor pulled his pledge to the stadium project, Kevin MacConnell—my very able Deputy AD who replaced Joe Quinlan when Joe was named the Director of Athletics and Recreational Services at Seton Hall University—and I went right back to seeking other avenues to help us finance the development.

We probably could have raised a good portion of the money to expand the stadium through a state-issued bond referendum as easily as a fundraising plan. However, some individuals and groups inside Rutgers felt uneasy about how taxpayers might react over mixing athletics with education. It seemed the university was always afraid of athletics and its potential to overshadow Rutgers's outstanding academic programs.

When Rutgers interviewed Courtney McAnuff to be the vice president for enrollment management, he made one request before accepting the position: he wanted to interview the AD. The AD, he said, was the key to his success as a senior-level administrator who recruited students. This statement certainly surprised many in "Old Queens."

Working with university administration and the office of the president, my team revised the stadium expansion budget to $102 million. We benefitted from having a wait-list for season tickets—more than 13,000 wanted to buy. We also anticipated that fewer than half of them would actually purchase season seats.

Once we were ready to go, however, the university informed us that we were required to use Rutgers Dining Services. Everything related to food had to be included in the $102 million.

This was a good arrangement. They were the only group that could get the club ready in time for the first game against Fresno State in 2008 in a new and expanded stadium. But using the dining services eliminated the up-front capital an outside vendor could put up.

I publicly committed to completing the project within the $102 million allocated, and we never spent one cent more.

While we reconciled these changes, Phil Furmanski, the Rutgers provost at the time, was helpful in wanting to keep the project on schedule.

Several times, President McCormick wanted to stop the project. First, he claimed we were working on it before the Board of Governors had approved it. Second, we had to schedule a public hearing on campus about the project before we could start.

The hearing actually turned out to be positive because most people, including the students attending the hearing, were enthusiastic supporters for its approval.

There were many issues along the way. Yet we successfully managed to stay on time and on budget. I went down to the stadium around midnight on Friday before the Fresno State game because the ironworkers were installing the seats in the club, and the schedule was tight. I wanted to make sure they were working through the night.

When I arrived, no one was working. I called the construction manager, ordered him to get the ironworkers back on the job, and stayed there until they came. I was determined that the club would be ready for the Monday night game, and it was.

We decided to put the students in the new end zone so we could give them more seating and create a more intense and energetic environment. This turned out to be a great move, and it was obvious at Rutgers's first-ever Big Ten home games against Penn State and Michigan in 2014. The club section sold out for the season opener versus Fresno State in 2008, and the largest Rutgers Stadium crowd prior to the 2014 Penn State game was there for the opener versus Cincinnati in 2009.

Expanding and remodeling Rutgers Stadium was essential to the football program's growth and emergence alongside the best competition of Division I sports. It was necessary if we were to participate in one of the five leading conferences of U.S. college athletics.

We imagined and wanted that to be the Big Ten. It was, and we were right to prepare for our entrance into this prestigious group of universities—national leaders both academically and athletically.

The strategy we created and executed, each partnership we formed, and every milestone we met by the time the new stadium opened were performed with the highest standards of management, business practices, oversight, and communications inside and outside the university.

It was and continues to be a magnificent accomplishment for Rutgers University and its proud and large family at home and around the country.

During this time, we also reviewed the basketball facilities. While we had HOK on-site during the stadium expansion, they reviewed the RAC. The problem was and continues to be the way the RAC was originally constructed—namely, with concrete and steel, which makes costs prohibitive for expansion, including seating and suites.

With Chris Paladino, president of DEVCO, we reviewed the potential for building a downtown arena and adjacent practice facilities. I visited other accommodations and realized that without the necessary help from the university to improve our basketball facility, we had to finish football first.

We did spend money in the RAC to improve both the men's and women's locker rooms. We also replaced some bench seating with chair-back seating on the home side for $1 million and developed and implemented the concept of courtside seats.

AREAS OF ONGOING CONCERN

Other issues continued to distract us. Two examples were the swimming and gymnastics facilities. Typical of the organizational confusion I encountered so often at Rutgers, the university allowed its recreation program to charge the swimming and diving teams rent to use their facilities.

The women's locker rooms in the swimming facility, the Werblin Center, were in disgraceful shape. I went to see them and realized that we had to spend the money to upgrade them. The problem was that no one could locate the agreement between the university and athletics for using the Werblin Center's Olympic pool. All the material we could find suggested that this would be a multiuse facility. No one in authority would intervene, so we did what we had to do. This is the type of frustration and confusion that we encountered and continues to plague Rutgers.

Issues surrounding gymnastics really frustrated us. Just as important was watching how often Rutgers was comfortable letting useless bureaucracy, red tape, and turf wars interfere with so many worthwhile student and university activities.

For many years, the Rutgers women's gymnastics team trained, practiced, and competed in the upstairs section, or "upper gym," of the College Avenue facility, which was managed by the Rutgers College Recreation staff.

One day, a staff person from the recreation department came to see Joe Quinlan. He was told that the gymnastics team needed to vacate the upper gym—remove all its equipment and find another place to practice and compete. "Why?" Joe asked. "What's the reason for forcing an official varsity team, composed of Rutgers students who regularly represent the university in competition, to completely uproot itself from normal operations?"

The answer he received was insensitive at best: "We've decided to use the space for other activities, and women's gymnastics has to go, period."

For several months, Joe and I held seemingly endless discussions with different university officials to find a location for the team. It was an exercise in continuous frustration and disbelief. Everyone cared *and* no one cared. If there was any reason to avoid helping us find a solution, somebody would come up with one.

Finally, the only remaining campus option was relocating to the Livingston College Recreation Center. That meant more exhausting discussions with academic deans. What surprised the university administrators the most? How much it cost the athletic department, the gymnastics program, and especially students and staff who raised money to pay the monthly rental for a venue.

Yet the poker-faced administrators were stoic. "Oh, well. This is merely the cost of doing business," they said.

How ironic that Chrystal Chollet-Norton, the outstanding women's gymnastics coach, was one of the most prolific fund-raisers in Division I intercollegiate athletics. She was also a tireless and strong advocate for her team. You'd think that would matter to Rutgers administrators and deans. It did not.

We eventually reached an agreement for the women's team to practice and compete in the Livingston College Recreation Center. The arrangement worked out well. We constructed a new vault pit with foam rubber padding and an elevated runway for all vaulting practices. It was a safer environment with enhanced equipment. The rental fee was substantial, but as Joe and I used to say with disbelief and a little sarcasm, "What's money to a public university, anyway?"

Looking back, university leaders weren't interested in helping the women's gymnastics team find a new, safe, and inexpensive place on campus to train and compete. Our athletic department had to go it alone, and we did. It was another sad example of Rutgers University being unable to connect all the dots and work as a unified organization.

When the university decided to float its $350 million bond issue, it could have easily put up an additional $50 million and asked donors to match it. It was, in my opinion, a valuable opportunity that Rutgers lost and ignored.

ATHLETICS AND ACADEMICS

Today, most American colleges and universities sponsoring athletic programs experience intense debates—sometimes out-and-out arguments—between advocates and opponents of intercollegiate sports.

Everyone acknowledges that winning football and basketball programs can generate millions of dollars of revenue for their schools. They disagree on how the monies are used: Which programs or groups benefit and which ones are neglected? What makes some university-based activities worthy of more subsidies coming from sports revenue?

Advocates believe that athletics promote pride among students, alumni, faculty, administrators and staff, families tied to the school, and the citizens of its home state. They feel that a university's athletic success and legacy, combined with academic excellence, raise application and enrollment rates. Many high school students want to attend schools where winning teams and conference championships stand right alongside distinguished academic programs.

Opponents have their own opinions. They are convinced that athletics undermine the quality and value of a college degree that student athletes—primarily football and basketball players—receive. That is, if these athletes even finish school.

One long-outspoken critic was Rutgers English professor William Dowling, author of *Confessions of a Spoilsport: My Life and Hard Times Fighting Sports Corruption at an Old Eastern University*.

Unfortunately, if he was looking for corruption, he should have started with the University of North Carolina and some of the SEC schools.

Dowling formed a group called Rutgers 1000, where he recruited others with similar negative feelings to rail with impunity against intercollegiate athletics. The organization's online slogan says, "Until Rutgers Is Set Free from Commercialized Div 1A Athletics."[4]

The group's mission was clear: they wanted to reduce the prominence of college athletics at major universities, starting with Rutgers.

Professor Dowling probably never read the athletics mission statement I developed when I became the AD, and he did not ask to discuss it with me. If he had read it, he could have understood the honor and pride of earning the third-highest national ranking in the NCAA's Academic Progress Report (APR) of all Division IA schools—after Navy and Stanford—which Rutgers received during my tenure. Moreover, by 2014, Rutgers football had ranked in the top 10 percent nationally in APR scores for six out of the past seven years.

Knowing this, Professor Dowling might have treated intercollegiate athletics and student athletes at Rutgers with more respect and less argument.

My team and I did our best to live up to the words in our mission statement:

> In accordance with the university's mission, the Division of Intercollegiate Athletics operates all of its programs in a manner consistent with the pursuit of intellectual inquiry, educational discovery, and academic success.
>
> The Division provides the personnel and program, including community service, necessary to enable student-athletes to pursue excellence in developing personal, academic, and athletic skills and, in so doing, supports the university in achieving its mission.

Prior to writing his *Confessions of a Spoilsport*, Dr. Dowling sent me several questions—allegedly so that my opinion would be included in the book. He also insisted on retaining the right to edit anything I might submit. I ignored his request.

The position of the Rutgers 1000 was in such unconditional opposition to college athletics that I saw no reason to respond to his offer. After Dowling published his book, the media often sought him out for quotes as an authority on the subject.

He held a rally once in front of Old Queens, a historic site on the university's main campus. On the way to a meeting on that end of campus, I had the chance to stop by and eyeball the number of demonstrators who attended—there were about 38, far short of a legion of opposition. No one would ever release how many members the group had, but it was significantly fewer than 1,000.

Professor Dowling would frequently send me letters, and on one occasion, he wrote me on a Monday after he went to Sunday Mass. "I assumed you heard the same gospel," he said. "Now would be a wonderful time to change your vision about what Rutgers athletics should be and come over to my side."

Opponents of college athletics will tell you that universities purposely steer revenue sport athletes toward majors that are void of any intellectual rigor, complex reasoning, and academic research. The pressure is higher for students on scholarship to take easy courses with little thinking or work required, they say. They believe that if practices, training, and team meetings take almost 40 hours a week of football and basketball players' time, then tough course loads will interfere with their performance on the field and the court.

Students arrive on scholarship to play their sport and earn a college education. Their success as student athletes depends very much on the leadership and commitment to academics presented by the university president, the AD, and the coaching staff.

Even while opponents saw me as an accessory to an imperfect system, I made a personal pledge to build a program that ensured that all our student athletes received the high-quality education that Rutgers offered *and* graduated. I was determined to reach that goal and shape winning programs and teams as well.

More than 99 percent of our student athletes will not play their sport professionally. Degrees from Rutgers would set the foundation for their future careers, earnings, and professional development. The metric that Rutgers and all other schools competing in the NCAA use to measure student athlete academics is the APR. Each academic term, the APR measures eligibility and retention for Division I student athletes.

Some background is important here. The NCAA developed the APR in 1990 to measure eventual graduation rates. At the time, national statistics indicated that a majority of student athletes were not graduating with sufficient qualifications or academic preparation for adult life. Universities and colleges were required to publish graduation rates after the Student Right-to-Know Act[5] was established.

Administrators and faculty wanted universities to hold athletes more accountable for academic success. The best way to do that, they said, was for schools to uphold the value of education more consistently and firmly.

The NCAA did not like what it saw either. Among student athletes who entered college between 1993 and 1996, 51 percent of football players graduated within six years, and only 41 percent of men's basketball players graduated.

The organization also came under increased pressure from leaders in academia to improve those dismal graduation rates. In 2004, the NCAA revised the APR so it would gauge student athletes' academic progress more closely and effectively.

Today, the APR measures scholarship athletes' academic performance term by term during the academic year. Each student athlete receiving some form of financial aid earns one retention point for staying in school and one point for maintaining academic eligibility. A team's total points are divided by points possible, then multiplied by 1,000 to give the APR.

Teams that fail to reach the NCAA's baseline calculation, established at 925, are subject to sanctions. There are three levels of penalties. At the first level, a team is limited to 16 hours of practice and competition time a week during a season instead of 20. The 4 hours lost must be used for academic activities. At the second level, reductions in competition in either the traditional or the off-season are applied. The third and final level of sanctions includes coaching suspensions, cuts in financial aid, and restricted NCAA membership. These concurrent penalties remain in place until the team's APR improves.

A prime example of this is the University of Connecticut, which was denied eligibility for the Big East and NCAA tournament in basketball during the 2012–2013 season for falling short in the APR—the year after they won the national championship.

At the other end of the spectrum, many of our coaching staff and players earned special recognition over the 2004–2009 period.

I was pleased with the APR scores that our football and men's and women's basketball teams earned from the 2004–2005 through the 2008–2009 seasons while I was the AD. The football team's scores started at 961 and increased each season to a score of 992. The men's basketball team scores ranged between 933 and 968, and the women's team scored between 946 and 968. There were a few teams that had to improve their academic record, and they did.

The APR is only one gauge of intercollegiate sports programs that raises strong-willed opinions about athletics versus academics. Advocates and adversaries also argue over graduation rates. Supporters respect student athletes playing in major conferences who are practically required to put in a minimum of 40 hours a week at their sport while they attend classes, maintain their academic course loads, and then graduate.

Critics point to poor graduation rates among football and men's and women's basketball players as proof of students failing at the central purpose of a college education—that is, building a strong foundation of knowledge and skills through intellectual rigor that prepares them to succeed in life. Each school has to look at how it approaches this subject. As the AD at Rutgers, I found common ground.

Graduation rates were as important as successful programs and winning seasons. I differed with the adversaries because they thought it was a straightforward principle. To them, either a student athlete graduates or does not, plain and simple.

Good programs ensure that most student athletes graduate. Critics are convinced that the student athlete who fails to graduate probably has little else to show for four years except maybe the distinction of playing in a championship or bowl game. Without a degree, they argue, the student will go nowhere fast.

APRs are calculated on a four-year rolling average. The four years ending in 2009 had Rutgers football ranked number one in Division I—ahead of Duke, Stanford, and the service academies. During this time, we appeared in five bowl games and won four bowl championships.

Still, judging any program's qualities based solely on graduation rates is neither clear-cut nor accurate. Accepting published graduation rates at face value can be misleading, and the NCAA's Division I Graduation Success Rate (GSR) is as murky as London's fog.

Specifically, student athletes transfer among schools. There might be legitimate family, financial, or other personal factors that influence them to leave the program. But they are counted as having left, and that's the problem with graduation rates and the APR. Some changes have been made to recognize the inherent problems in the old calculations.

There are also student athletes who talk and act like prima donnas. They believe their performance on the field or court should guarantee a starting position every time they put on a game uniform. When some of them wake up and find out they lost their spot to another player, they want to be "released" so they can transfer and play for another school.

Now they are dealing with other issues. A different university might not accept all their credits during transfer, which will delay their graduation. They also have to prove themselves as athletes working with unfamiliar coaches, unknown teammates, and a different system in a new university culture.

Did the university, the coaches, or the athletic program where the athlete began fail in their responsibilities if the student did not successfully graduate there or at another institution? Not necessarily, and maybe not at all.

Some collegiate football or basketball players expect college to be a one-way ticket to professional sports and getting rich fast. That can and does happen for a very limited number of college athletes, and some might consider that a great achievement. But the overwhelming majority who make sport their sole reason for attending college are misguided, sometimes delusional, and often disappointed. The chances of reaching the pro ranks are slim. Few are invited to try out, and even fewer ever put on a uniform for game day.

At Rutgers, I urged our coaching staff to emphasize to their student athletes that attending college and earning a degree is a unique gift. For some who struggled in high school academically, it is a privilege. All the coaches agreed and felt as strongly about it as I did.

The opportunity to accomplish athletic excellence is a tremendous benefit and priceless experience in life. Getting a superior education and graduating, plus being part of an accomplished athletic program, are always my preferred goals for student athletes.

My team and I firmly believed in and practiced that philosophy at Rutgers, and the outcomes we realized brought pride to our programs and to the university. In the 2007–2008 academic year, 17 student athletes earned a perfect 4.0 GPA for the fall term, and 26 others received the same honor for the 2008 spring term. During that period, 43 student athletes recorded a perfect 4.0 GPA in at least one semester.

Brandon Renkart, who was a standout linebacker for Coach Greg Schiano's team, received the Robert A. Simms National Scholar-Athlete Award at the 60th annual NFF and College Hall of Fame dinner. Simms, himself a former Rutgers scholar athlete and standout football player, had endowed the scholarship.

Brandon earned a BS in engineering—a demanding academic program anywhere—from one of the country's leading university engineering schools. He had to miss one practice day a week for labs. He was one of 16 national scholar athletes honored at the annual College Hall of Fame black-tie dinner at the Waldorf Astoria Hotel.

It was the second consecutive year in which a Rutgers player received a major national academic and athletic award. Brandon's teammate, running back Brian Leonard, received the Campbell Trophy, also known as the "Academic Heisman" in 2006. It goes annually to an individual who demonstrates exceptional achievement for academic success, football performance, and exemplary community leadership.

An undergraduate major in labor and employment relations, Brian was one of the most feared backfield blockers and versatile backs in college football during his career. He earned Academic All-Conference honors three times and a place on ESPN's Academic All-District Team in 2005. In 2006, Brian also became Rutgers's sixth National Scholar-Athlete Award winner and the first since 2003.

Brian was selected in the second round of the 2007 NFL draft by the St. Louis Rams, where he played in the 2007 and 2008 season. Next he wore the Cincinnati Bengals uniform from 2009 to 2012. In 2013, he joined the Tampa Bay Buccaneers and played again for Greg Schiano.

Another outstanding student scholar athlete was Nate Jones, a finance major and defensive back who was also honored at the Hall of Fame dinner in New York in 2002. Nate went on to have a fine NFL career, playing for the Cowboys, Dolphins, Broncos, and Patriots.

Rutgers football had three national scholar athletes during Coach Schiano's tenure, building on what the university had achieved in the past with national standout players, such as Alex Kroll and Bob Simms.

Alex Kroll was named to seven All-American teams in 1961 while he played at Rutgers and earned academic distinction as a Henry Rutgers Scholar. Later he played professionally for the American Football League's then New York Titans, which became the New York Jets. After leaving professional football, he embarked on a distinguished business career that led to serving as the chief executive officer of Young & Rubicam, a prominent worldwide advertising firm.

After graduating from Rutgers, Bob Simms played professional football for the New York Giants and Pittsburgh Steelers. Later he became a successful investment banker and fellow board member at the NFF and College Hall of Fame.

My attention and my loyalties were never limited to building the football and basketball programs. I admired every one of our student athletes.

And many of them who competed on our Olympic sport teams distinguished themselves and honored Rutgers in academics as often as they did in competition.

I remember who they were and how proud I was of them.

Rutgers senior rower Melanie Spero earned the honor and invitation to deliver the undergraduate commencement address for Rutgers's 2008 graduation exercises.

Nina Montero, a defender on the women's soccer team, was selected to ESPN's Academic All-District II First Team with a GPA of over 3.8 in English, her major.

Our women's tennis team earned all-academic honors from the Intercollegiate Tennis Association. Four of the team's athletes received ITA Scholar-Athlete Awards and maintained GPAs of 3.5 and higher.

A final thought about our graduation rates. More than 100 of our student athletes earned degrees in 2008. Rutgers conferred degrees on more than 100 of its graduating athletes during each of my last four years and well over 550 since 2004. Rutgers's commencement in 2008 included twice as many student athlete graduates as in 2003 with six fewer sports.

CHAPTER 5

THE DON IMUS
INCIDENT

On April 4, 2007, Rutgers athletics, and the university alongside it, became the lead story across network and cable news. This was one of the most controversial and provocative incidents on a national scale in the school's history.

It also raised questions about moral decency and human character.

On a Wednesday morning following the Rutgers women's basketball team's participation in the national championship game against Tennessee in Cleveland, WFAN Radio and MSNBC, its simulcast partner, which televised its daily program *Imus in the Morning* with syndicated radio talk show host Don Imus, made provocative and controversial comments about our team, with Imus taking the lead. Imus had been around a long time. Millions of faithful listeners knew exactly what to expect from him and his sidekicks. Imus and company delivered their familiar in-your-face opinions about anything and everything going on in America and the world—occasionally with sober analysis but mainly with raunchy humor and humiliating sarcasm at someone else's expense.

Sports announcer Sid Rosenberg reported the results of the previous night's game between Rutgers and Tennessee. Then in a comment about Rutgers's team of eight African American and two white players, Rosenberg said, "The more I look at Rutgers, they look exactly like the Toronto Raptors [of the NBA]." Right after his comment, Imus's executive producer, Bernard

McGuirk, jumped in and referred to the game as a "Spike Lee thing," adding, "The Jigaboos versus the Wannabees—that movie that he had."[1]

But then it grew even more insulting and more humiliating—all live on national radio and TV. McGuirk called the Rutgers players "hard-core hos." Then Imus, who was comfortable crossing the line separating acceptable on-air humor from degrading statements about different classes of people—often minorities—followed McGuirk's remark and called the women "nappy-headed hos."

At the time, American culture didn't use the expression *going viral* to describe outrageous events spreading instantly and widely on social media. Still, what happened that morning went viral in every way it could. It created shockwaves. Network evening news anchors at ABC, NBC, CBS, CNN, MSNBC, and Fox made Imus's remarks their lead story.

That same Wednesday morning, the team players, Head Coach Vivian Stringer, and my wife, Terry, and I, boarded a plane in Cleveland and headed home. Though they lost, the women played a terrific game and had a tremendous NCAA tournament. We planned to celebrate their outstanding season the following night at the RAC.

Thursday evening, I heard some rumblings about the Imus remark, but everyone was cheering at the rally. The following day was Good Friday, and most everyone went home for Easter. Those rumblings went viral over the weekend.

On Saturday evening, Terry and I went to church to participate in the Easter Vigil celebration. There were two voice mail messages for me when I returned home. One was from popular sports radio talk show host Mike Francesa. The other was from Imus himself.

Francesa's message said, "Bob, please talk to me before you talk to Imus," so I called him. He told me that Imus wanted to come to Rutgers and apologize personally to the women. Mike thought we could get Imus to establish a scholarship at Rutgers. It could be one measure of penance for the disgraceful remarks he and members of his program had made less than 48 hours earlier.

Don Imus found himself in the middle of a firestorm he encouraged and created. It spread so fast across national media that you could have said it was his personal "s***storm." That's precisely what it was. Because of his sick sense of humor, Imus and his program found themselves in the middle of an extraordinary scandal from which neither he nor CBS, his network sponsor, could escape.

I hung up with Francesa and called Imus. He said, "I'd like to come and apologize to the team." I replied, "Don, I have to ask the players if they are willing to see you. I'll call a meeting with the team and Coach Stringer and her staff on Monday. It's entirely up to the women whatever happens next, no matter what you're asking them to agree to." It was not his call, and I told him that.

On Easter Sunday, I spent most of the day making phone calls. One of the first calls I made was to Governor Jon Corzine. I asked the governor to come to the RAC on Monday—not to make an official public statement but to address the team and affirm that he and the state of New Jersey stood firmly with the women and their principles. Next, following the advice of my longtime friend Harold Hodes, I called Steve DeMicco, a highly regarded political and marketing strategist, and asked him to meet me on Monday as well. We would discuss how we would handle the media from that day forward.

My final calls were to Rutgers president Richard McCormick and the Reverend Dr. DeForest B. "Buster" Soaries, a prominent African American spiritual leader and former Secretary of State of New Jersey. I asked both men to attend the meeting.

The mood at the gathering was tense. Everyone's feelings were fragile. Imus's program had attacked every fiber of their self-respect.

I informed the women's team of Imus's request to meet with them and personally apologize. After some discussion, they agreed to see him. First, though, I suggested—and they agreed—that we would hold a press conference. Rutgers athletics, and in particular these women, would have their say about this incident before anyone sat down with Imus.

I felt it was the responsibility of the AD to protect the student athletes in situations like this.

Less than 24 hours after the incident became national news, local and national newspaper reporters, plus TV correspondents and news crews, started camping outside and inside the RAC. Steve and I agreed on a strategy for the following day's media event.

Governor Corzine came on Monday afternoon and spoke to the players. He also offered Drumthwacket, the governor's official residence in Princeton, as a place for the team to meet with Imus.

Coach Stringer and I asked two players—Heather Zurich, who was white, and Essence Carson, who was black—to go to their dorm rooms and write personal remarks stating exactly how they felt.

On April 10, 2007, at 11:00 a.m., I opened the press conference at the RAC. Joining the team members on stage with me were Coach Stringer and President McCormick. Stacey Brann, the women's basketball contact for the sports information office and an excellent sports media professional, moderated the proceedings. Media representatives filled the room, including then NBC News anchor Brian Williams and CNN's Soledad O'Brien.

My remarks were relatively brief but definitely clear about what we wanted everyone in the state and the country to understand:

The real story was the 2006–2007 Rutgers women's basketball team—their incredible achievements, where they came from, and how far they went to play in the pinnacle of their sport, the NCAA national championship game—and not the despicable and degrading comments made by Don Imus and his producer.

Their radio program, also shown on national television, abused the unique privilege to broadcast that they received. Their words assassinated the character of 10 exceptionally talented and hard-working young women, among the very best who proudly represented their school; their classmates; fellow student athletes; and Rutgers alumni around the world on a national stage.

The episode has to stand as a powerful reminder to everybody that making humiliating remarks that degrade and harm others who are innocent has consequences.

After I finished, Coach Stringer spoke, followed by President McCormick. Then Heather Zurich and Essence Carson made their personal statements. Each young woman described the deep insult they felt from Imus and McGuirk's callous words and the unanimous pride and dignity every player on the women's team shared as student athletes representing Rutgers University. "The Rutgers University women's basketball team has made history," said Essence, then a junior forward. "We haven't done anything to deserve this controversy, and yet it has taken a toll on us mentally and physically."[2]

They were terrific. They exemplified the best in student athletes and the high quality of student athletes we had at Rutgers.

Members of the media had time to speak briefly with Heather, Essence, and three other veterans on the team—Kia Vaughan, Matee Ajavon, and Katie Adams—before they left the RAC to go to their classes. Coach Stringer, President McCormick, and I also remained to answer more questions.

Two days later, on the evening of April 12, the team was ready to meet with Imus at the governor's mansion in Princeton. Governor Corzine said he would be there.

Looking back on that awkward moment, I think it was the only way for the women and Rutgers to put the incident behind us. Yet we all knew it would never totally disappear from our memories. The whole thing was too outrageous to forget.

As I boarded the bus with the team Thursday evening, my cell phone rang with the news that something unexpected and potentially tragic had happened. The state police called. Governor Corzine's security detail was driving him back from the southern part of the state on the way to our meeting when his SUV was involved in a bad accident. He was critically injured. His orders were for us to go ahead and meet Imus at Drumthwacket without him.

The bus ride was quiet. Everyone was naturally apprehensive. No one really knew what to expect from Imus. After all, he had built his career on "talk radio," where he could come across as an empathetic Dr. Jekyll one minute, then launch into his Mr. Hyde routine of humiliating put-downs the next.

When we arrived at the governor's residence, a swarm of media was waiting. We had also told the players they could invite their parents, and some families chose to come. Once inside, we proceeded to the library.

Finally, Don Imus, accompanied by his wife, Deirdre, arrived in a stretch limo. We asked Reverend Soaries to moderate the meeting. He made some opening remarks about the unusual importance and meaning of the occasion for everyone who was there. Imus looked uncomfortable, and it seemed appropriate. He was lucky those young women were willing to be in the same room with him.

At last, Imus spoke. He reflected on all the work he did on behalf of charities, such as his ranch in New Mexico for kids with cancer and fundraising work for children's hospitals.

No one wanted to hear any of this except Don. I think his wife realized that he didn't understand the point of the meeting and she interrupted, paying compliments to the women players and their achievements.

Don did finally apologize. WFAN radio and MSNBC also issued apologies and called what happened deplorable.

The evening's events were emotionally intense, and I'm sure everybody present still remembers every detail. I certainly do. One very personal comment stands out for me. A stately gentleman of color and grandfather of one of the players stood up and said, "Mr. Imus, I'm the son of sharecroppers from South Carolina. When I was six years old, I worked on a worm farm. The white boss out in the fields told me I had to do something that humiliated me. He said if I didn't do it, he'd kick me. Then he called me the N-word. I want you to know what it feels like to be unaccepted."

By this time, Imus appeared visibly affected by the statements he had heard from the female players and others present. He appeared to understand the consequences of what he had done.

As the meeting ended, there were some hugs between the players and Deirdre Imus. She was crying, and so were some of the women. I stayed behind for a few minutes for a short meeting with Coach Stringer, Reverend Soaries, and the players.

Reverend Soaries was a helpful partner for us in handling the situation. He also supported us by serving as a spokesperson on TV. I was under pressure from the Reverends Al Sharpton and Jesse Jackson, who both wanted to get involved, and I did not want that kind of spectacle. The women trusted Reverend Soaries's advice and counsel. I did too. He was, and remains, a good friend.

In the end, a few of the players considered suing Imus. At least two groups of parents hired lawyers to discuss a lawsuit. I met with Jonathan Alger, Rutgers general counsel and now president of James Madison University. I also told the players I would not stand in their way if they chose to take legal action against Imus or his staff. But I cautioned them to think carefully about it because things in their personal lives that they wanted to remain private could be exposed to the public in a lawsuit. Imus or McGuirk could file countersuits. The situation could become very nasty with investigations and depositions, and corporate lawyers could drag the process on for years. Finally, Coach Stringer discouraged them from suing Imus, McGuirk, and the two networks.

That experience served as a lesson for everyone involved. CBS had fired Imus on April 12, prior to his meeting with the team that night. MSNBC had dropped its simulcast of the program a day before, on April 11. His program was worth approximately $15 million in annual revenue for CBS.

Some believe Imus has nine lives. His radio show returned to the airwaves when he signed a deal with Sirius Radio not long after the incident. But I believe he was permanently and professionally crippled by his words and the atmosphere he created. I am also proud and grateful for the class with which the players, coaches, and university handled the situation.

The national embarrassment over Imus's racial insults against the Rutgers women's basketball team happened 12 years ago. How does it matter now? Today's undergraduates were just kids at the time. Most don't know who Imus is, and few have ever listened to the shock jock's radio program.

But it matters because people in our midst still commit insidious acts of bigotry, sexual assault, and other unspeakable crimes against young people—including vulnerable student athletes.

Were Imus's words of intolerance less offensive than Larry Nassar's sexual assaults against female gymnasts over more than two decades while he was the USA Gymnastics team doctor and an osteopathic physician at Michigan State University? No, they were not. Nassar's crimes came to light in 2017 because his courageous victims believed they could speak out and stop him.

What about the 2018 revelations that Dr. Richard Strauss, a former team doctor for Ohio State University's wrestling team, molested and behaved inappropriately toward Buckeye wrestlers between 1986 and 1994? And what about Jerry Sandusky, who sexually molested and psychologically scarred countless adolescent boys while he coached football at Penn State?

Imus, Nassar, Strauss, and Sandusky: their acts showed an alarming indifference toward moral decency and human character as athletic coaches, sports physicians, and media personalities. Scholastic and university ADs are trusted with managing processes—with vigilance—that attempt to prevent and, when reasonably possible, protect student athletes from becoming victims.

CHAPTER 6

UPHOLDING
TRADITIONS

I often thought that traditions surrounding the athletic program were missing at Rutgers. One day while sitting in the stadium with Joe Quinlan and Kevin MacConnell, I looked at the concrete and said, "We have to paint it red." (Actually, we painted it scarlet for the Scarlet Knights.) We also painted the RAC and put the block *R* logo everywhere we could. We did much more to foster tradition around athletics, like encouraging our fans to wear red to all of the games they attended.

The block *R* logo became an interesting topic and issue. The administration said it was only a "spirit mark," and the university would have its own logo, for which it spent $500,000 with a Chicago firm to create a script *R*. Coach Greg Schiano had a wonderful idea for increasing public recognition of the block *R*, and Kevin marketed them throughout the tristate area on cars and T-shirts.

We created the Scarlet Walk, where a statue of a football player representing the first college football game between Rutgers and Princeton stands just outside the stadium's main entrance. Two hours before kickoff, the team buses drop off the Scarlet Knights at the top of the Scarlet Walk, and the team members head down the brick path to the locker room with the Rutgers band while throngs of fans greet and encourage them.

Bob speaking at the Insight Bowl pep rally in Scottsdale, Arizona, December 2005.

Greg Schiano approached me about the mailing address of the stadium, which used to be Frelinghuysen Avenue. I managed to get it changed to One Scarlet Way, and the U.S. Postal Service approved it.

We started a tradition of taking the Marching Scarlet Knights to one regular season away game and to all bowl games as a reward for their hard work and impressive dedication. The athletic department paid for the band's expenses on those trips.

I could not understand why we had to be responsible for the band while the university had the Mason Gross School of the Arts supporting all areas of the fine and performing arts. One year we spent $90,000 to buy new tubas for the band, and we also bought new uniforms. Curiously, the band was part of the athletic department budget.

I still enjoy watching the band's impressive halftime performances. But it's time for Rutgers to appropriate more funding for the Mason Gross

School so it can support the marching band's continued growth. They deserve every opportunity to perform with the same excellence as other legendary Big Ten school bands. They should be invited to march in various events around the state. The exposure would be terrific for Rutgers. Another ideal place for them to perform would be the Macy's Thanksgiving Day Parade in New York City.

We started the tradition of having both the Rutgers University Police and the New Jersey State Police accompany the football team and head coach, as most big-time programs do. The New Jersey State Police used it as a recruiting tool. When we went to the NCAA Women's Basketball Final Four in Cleveland, the state police sent two female troopers to accompany Coach Stringer and the team.

Greg thought up a slogan, "Keep Chopping," and even registered it as a trademark. The first year, he received $5,000 in revenue, which he planned to donate to the Special Olympics, but the university said he could not accept the money unless he turned it over to the school. Greg still has the check in his drawer. It is a sad commentary. Each year at the New Jersey Special Olympics competition, the Rutgers football team joins in the march of athletes to start the competition—a tradition continued and properly expanded by Schiano's successors, Kyle Flood and Chris Ash.

It is important for people who are connected with and admire Rutgers to understand that my team and I tried to build a complete program. We worked tirelessly to create an environment that brought pride to the school and a feeling of satisfaction among all students and alumni. We held a pep rally the night before each season's first home game, and Coach Schiano and team members would also stop by. Members and coaches from athletics teams, including football and basketball players, participated in the annual Rutgers Dance Marathon and were present for "Rutgers Day" in the spring.

Students constantly thanked us for giving them the opportunity to speak with optimism and pride about their school. Strangers who recognize me still come up to thank me for what we did at Rutgers.

The chapter, which describes the key challenges my staff faced when we arrived at Rutgers, implies there were more problems than victories. That's not entirely true. While tackling challenges and setting a new direction for athletics, we also celebrated some wonderful events that will live forever with pride and joy in our memories.

They were unforgettable milestones on our path to success. First was Rutgers football's invitation to the Insight Bowl in 2005. It was the first bowl game the school ever played in outside of New Jersey and the second one in university history.

The people who ran the Insight Bowl also managed the Fiesta Bowl, which made the Insight Bowl a first-class operation. And as I grew to expect and admire Coach Schiano, I saw how he planned every detail of the bowl trip with meticulous care, including who was invited, who would sit where, and who would share a room at the hotel.

When the team arrived at Newark Airport for our flight, we received a send-off tribute with fire engines and hoses. When we landed in Phoenix, the Insight Bowl Committee rolled a red carpet out to our plane. Phoenix police riding motorcycles escorted us to our hotel, where a band greeted us. It was an exciting feeling every place we went. We always felt welcome.

Added to all that was learning that Brent Musburger, one of TV's top college football announcers, had been named the play-by-play broadcaster for our game.

The football players enjoyed the hotel because it was all Rutgers, with a swimming pool in the middle surrounded by their rooms.

Most meaningful were the Rutgers fans who came from across the country to show their support. Their excitement was something to behold, and I will never forget it. At the pregame pep rally and function with the team, I felt a tremendous sense of accomplishment and communion with the Rutgers family. Even President McCormick stood up with me and rallied the crowd.

Christmas also fell during the time we were in Phoenix, and we wanted to make sure the Christmas season would be truly special for everyone who was with us.

On Christmas Eve, John Ternyila, who worked tirelessly as part of the finance department, dressed up as Santa. Two of my daughters reluctantly dressed up as elves and were terrific. We invited all the youngsters of the coaches to a reading of *The Night before Christmas*, which I was pleased to present.

When I finished, all of us in the room heard bells ringing, and Santa appeared. Each child sat on his lap and received a gift brought and wrapped by their families. But we didn't stop at Christmas Eve. On Christmas Day—and with the help of Scott Asher from the Insight Bowl Committee, who has become a good friend—my wife, Terry, arranged for a Mass at one of the hotel's meeting rooms, fully accompanied by Christmas music.

The game, which was a thriller, was our opportunity to surprise the nation with our performance. The late James Gandolfini, the celebrated Rutgers alumnus and award-winning actor of HBO's famous series *The Sopranos*, stood at midfield along with Greg Brown, CEO of Motorola, and our team captains for the official coin toss.

It was a gathering of New Jerseyans that everyone will always remember with pride.

The second and most memorable event was the night game at home in 2006 against Louisville, who were ranked number three nationally at the time. Both teams were undefeated. It did more than give Rutgers great exposure on national prime time TV; I believe it was the one game that turned Rutgers football around.

Everything came together that night. During the summer of 2006, I was playing in Yogi Berra's annual celebrity golf classic at the Montclair Golf Club. Mike Francesa and Chris "Mad Dog" Russo of New York's WFAN radio were broadcasting live. Their *Mike and the Mad Dog* program was the highest-rated sports talk show in the nation. They grabbed me between the ninth and tenth holes for an interview. I made up my mind to ask them, while they were broadcasting live and without warning, to broadcast their show from Rutgers Stadium. The game I suggested: Louisville.

Feeling like they had no way out, they agreed.

Meanwhile, Kevin MacConnell's friend and former AD at Temple, Charlie Theokas, knew the manager of the Empire State Building. With Charlie's help, Kevin got the manager to agree to light up one of America's historic buildings in Rutgers's colors during the game.

Harold Hodes, who served on the boards for the New Jersey Turnpike Authority and the Garden State Parkway, intervened on our behalf, and signs on both highways lit up with scarlet and white on the night of the game.

Mother Nature cooperated and provided us with an uncommonly warm November evening. Earlier in the week, the sense of anticipation around the campus was palpable. Students waited in line at night to get their tickets, and Coach Schiano bought pizza for them.

The way we finished the game—with a late field goal by Jeremy Ito that capped a furious second-half comeback for a 28–25 win—inspired thousands of students and fans to rush the field when the clock ran out. With that victory, Rutgers jumped to number six in the nation. It was a night that everyone associated with Rutgers will always think about as absolutely magical.

Like many things that happened in my life, I really could not internalize the success. But after congratulating Coach Schiano, his dedicated staff, and of course, the players, I went home with Terry because I didn't know what to do with myself.

I have often watched replays of the game and realized how brilliant the defense was in the second half. The calls Coach Schiano made were on target.

On the eve of the Louisville game, Jerry Izenberg of the *Newark Star Ledger* interviewed Big East Commissioner Mike Tranghese, and among his many statements, the following stood out:

The ironic part of this football fairy tale is that all along, the weakest sister of all (once Temple left)—the weakest team and the worst ad for a reborn Big East according to the deserting trio, the conference that lured all three and a number of other leagues—would emerge as a nationally ranked team.

Who would have thought that Rutgers—in the longest hibernation in American major college football—would awaken, crawl out of the cave and become a force with which to be reckoned?

Mike Tranghese—that's who.

I had begun to think that Rutgers could become our ace in the hole even though nobody else did. I like the things Bob (Mulcahy) was doing. And I liked what I started to see when Greg Schiano came in. The program they took over was in deplorable condition. Rutgers football was terrible.

But I watched Greg and I liked what I saw. He kept working. It didn't matter whether they won or lost in the beginning—and they lost a lot—but he kept on working.

I knew they were going to get better. . . . Better in the classrooms, better in the facilities, better in the kind of recruits Greg was getting. Now it had to get better on the field. And when it happened, I was happy for Rutgers. Mulcahy and Schiano earned this. They did this. They achieved it.[1]

The impact of the game I subsequently understood.

Looking back, I wish I had gone to downtown New Brunswick to watch the sheer joy on the faces of thousands of Rutgers students and supporters as they cheered. It was a special moment, and I'm not sure it can ever be duplicated—unless Rutgers wins the national championship.

Finally, I am very proud of several milestones our athletic programs reached in the decade I was the AD.

Greg Schiano was the unanimous choice of five national organizations as the college football coach of the year in 2006 as well as the Big East coach of the year. The women's basketball team reached the Final Four twice, and Head Coach Vivian Stringer was inducted into the James Naismith Memorial Basketball Hall of Fame as well as the Women's Basketball Hall of Fame.

Bob appearing on *Mike and the Mad Dog* just before number-15 Rutgers defeated number-3 Louisville, November 9, 2006.

Jim Stagnitta was named the nation's coach of the year in men's lacrosse. Coach Mike Mulqueen's outdoor track-and-field team won its first conference championship. And Head Coach Fred Hill's varsity baseball teams won three conference championships, made several NCAA appearances, and delivered stars like Todd Frazier and David DeJesus to the major leagues.

They were special times that have come to reflect the spirit and strength of our department and its people.

The city of New Brunswick finally started looking and feeling like a college town as our vision for athletics developed and flourished. I don't think it was coincidental.

Johnson & Johnson's urban renewal program, New Brunswick Tomorrow, began in the 1980s and revitalized some of the city's long-deteriorating residential and retail areas. New stores and restaurants brought additional merchants and more customers. Thousands of new condominiums and townhouses attracted more affluent individuals and families who made New Brunswick their home.

Yet hundreds of banners prominently displaying the Rutgers *R* appeared throughout the town soon after the university's athletic teams started winning conference championships and bowl games. From merchants, residents, and city and county employees to students, faculty, and administrators, anyone with a connection to Rutgers was proud and wanted to be associated with the school.

Rutgers and its home city waited decades for that feeling to exist. It finally arrived in the late 1990s and 2000s, when Rutgers student athletes started competing and winning on much tougher fields and courts of play than at any time in the school's history.

During this time, applications for admission, SAT scores, and fundraising all increased.

One thing we sorely lacked was a traditional rival. Now that Rutgers is a member of the Big Ten Conference, I believe it should be Penn State. We need to create a trophy that we compete for. My suggestion would be a replica of the Durham boat showing George Washington and his troops crossing the Delaware from Pennsylvania to Trenton for the battle that changed the tide of the Revolutionary War. It symbolizes the historic relationship between the two states. Emanuel Gottlieb Leutze's 1851 oil painting *Washington Crossing the Delaware* is one of the most revered pieces of art in U.S. history.

Rutgers has always been an outstanding university. It was something special to witness its athletic teams earning repeated acclaim on a national stage, with thousands of alumni, students, and others bursting with long-awaited pride. Even more special was being a part of it.

CHAPTER 7

CONFERENCES

THE BIG EAST AND THE BIG TEN

BIG EAST CONFERENCE REALIGNMENT

Conference realignment came to the forefront in the 1990s. Many traced the movement of schools back to Penn State's decision to "leave the East" and accept membership to the Big Ten in 1990. Rutgers joined the Big East Football Conference in 1991 and upgraded to full membership in 1995.

An issue with the Big East membership began to surface in February 2003 at the Big East ADs' meeting in New York. The University of Miami had a special deal with the conference, which guaranteed the school $9 million in annual revenue. But the school always seemed to complain about one thing or the other, including what they saw as biased officiating. Added to that was Miami president Donna Shalala's failure to remember her commitment to Big East commissioner Mike Tranghese and Miami's pledge to remain in the league. At the conference's annual meeting in Florida in May that same year, the realignment issue broke out in the open. Miami said they were going to the ACC, and Boston College and Syracuse said they would follow if invited. Dick Weiss, a terrific reporter who covered college athletics for the *New York Daily News*, reported that both Boston College and Miami University met secretly with the ACC commissioner. ADs in the league didn't know anything about it at the time.

Virginia Tech said they were committed to stay, although I later found out they tried to get an invitation to the ACC but were denied. Three votes could block any invitation, and North Carolina, Duke, and Virginia all opposed Virginia Tech's entry.

This created a difficult situation for all the ADs because we enjoyed not only strong business relationships but also trusting friendships with each other. Politics also reared up as the governor of Virginia put pressure on the University of Virginia trustees to change their vote and accept Virginia Tech into the ACC, which they did.

The Big East's annual end-of-year meetings took place at Ponte Vedra, Florida, in May 2003. These emotional proceedings were held while hordes of press waited outside the conference room. The first movements were Virginia Tech and Miami going to the ACC, effective in 2004.

Many predicted the demise of the Big East, but the ADs set up a special committee of four ADs and six university presidents who would work over the summer of 2004 to reconstruct the league. They would rewrite the bylaws before any new members were invited.

The key members on the committee were Phil Austin, president of the University of Connecticut; Mark Nordenberg, chancellor of the University of Pittsburgh; David Hardesty, president of West Virginia University; and Buzz Shaw, chancellor of Syracuse University. These four leaders all had experience with NCAA committees, and they helped us negotiate our new bylaws. They understood the value of the Big East Conference and worked together with the ADs in ways that subsequent conference presidents did not.

The two football ADs were Jake Crouthamel from Syracuse and myself. The two basketball ADs from Seton Hall and Georgetown were Jeff Fogelson and Joe Lang. Father Leahy, president of Boston College, and Jack DeGioia, president of Georgetown University, completed the committee.

Several meetings over the summer of 2004 resulted in a revised set of bylaws with a $5 million penalty if anyone left.

Everyone agreed to the new bylaws, which included a procedure that allowed football and basketball programs to separate from the conference in an orderly fashion if it ever came to that.

All of a sudden, after participating all summer in the discussions to remake the league, Boston College announced in August that it was defecting to the ACC and would not pay the $5 million penalty. On that same day, the letter from Boston AD Gene DeFillipo was still on the Eagles' athletics website proclaiming the school's allegiance and commitment to the Big East. It was obvious the school had been working behind the scenes to orchestrate their departure. That decision represented the kinds of difficulties and battles we fought. Boston College ultimately did pay the penalty.

During this period, I saw relationships grow stronger among the ADs of the schools who remained loyal to the conference. They had to trust one another, and they did. I also saw how ADs who preferred to work alone struggled. Several ADs from that era believed the conference would have survived if their leadership had remained united and supported the best interests of its member schools.

I kept a letter that Mike Tranghese, Big East Conference commissioner, sent to member ADs and university presidents on July 24, 2003. The subject was expansion protocol. Following a conference meeting at Newark Airport, Mike provided "the tenets of an expansion protocol process that would allow us to proceed in an orderly and proper manner."

These thoughtful and fair tenets included the following:

- Prior to discussions about specific potential expansion candidates, the Big East Conference would decide its own future structure first.
- As the process for selecting schools developed and the conference identified institutions as good candidates, their own commissioners would be discreetly notified.
- Before making any formal contracts with those candidate institutions, their respective commissioner again would be notified before any public announcement.

During my tenure, I always admired Mike's leadership and professionalism. He demonstrated the finest qualities of building consensus and harmony among the ADs and their schools. He fought for what was best for the conference and was a nationally respected figure. Mike's strong relationships with other conference commissioners allowed the Big East to remain a member of the BCS. He was respected by everyone in college sports.

HISTORICAL PERSPECTIVE ABOUT CONFERENCES

By the mid-1990s, Rutgers football had come a long way from its traditional past when it played the likes of Lehigh, Lafayette, and Colgate. Rutgers had enjoyed some hard-fought games and a lot of student and alumni support, particularly the 100th anniversary football game between Rutgers and Princeton in 1969, which Rutgers won 29–0 at home. That game was and will forever be a salient moment in Rutgers's history. It provided a magnificent opportunity to celebrate what college football has become in American life. It would have been appropriate for Rutgers and Princeton to play the 150th Anniversary Game at Yankee Stadium, which they were welcomed to do. Unfortunately, Rutgers declined the invitation.

In 1979, Rutgers declined an invitation to join the Big East when it was just a basketball conference, thus opening the door for in-state rival Seton Hall to accept membership. Then while competing in the Eastern Eight, Rutgers didn't feel comfortable abandoning Penn State and moving its basketball program to the Big East with Providence, St. Johns, Georgetown, Syracuse, Boston College, Seton Hall, and Connecticut, with Villanova and Pittsburgh joining soon after.

Rutgers remained in the Eastern Eight, which eventually became the Atlantic 10 (A-10) Conference. The A-10 was primarily a basketball conference, and its logo was a basketball. Rutgers remained resolved to find a home in an "all-sports" conference—one that included football.

Things remained static until 1991, when the Big East started sponsoring football. The University of Miami became a full member, and Rutgers accepted an invitation to join as a football-only member along with

Temple, Virginia Tech, and West Virginia. Four years later in 1995, the conference upgraded Rutgers and West Virginia to full membership. Rutgers had finally achieved its goal of competing in an "all-sports" league.

When I took over in 1998, Rutgers still yearned for its flagship athletic programs in football and men's and women's basketball and soccer to compete against some of the country's toughest and most prestigious teams.

At least by this point, the football team played Miami, Virginia Tech, and Pittsburgh regularly instead of Cornell and Columbia. Men's basketball took the court against teams like Georgetown, Connecticut, St. John's, and Villanova. And the women's basketball team reached the NCAA Mideast Regional Semifinals against top-seeded, unbeaten, and defending national champion Tennessee.

If Rutgers really expected to become a viable competitor in college sports, it had to advance to one of the NCAA's top-ranked conferences and claim its seat at the table. The eventual reshuffling of the Big East Conference diminished some of the classic rivalries for Rutgers when teams like Boston College, Syracuse, and Pittsburgh departed for the ACC.

There were other issues too. Realigning the conference to accommodate changes required the addition of Louisville, South Florida, and Cincinnati. Football was possible because the basketball programs in the conference decided to go along with it. The basketball schools could have vetoed the realignment, but they did not. The basketball schools supported it.

There was a strong spirit of cooperation to demonstrate that a 16-team conference could work. It did for a few years until more serious shifts started to happen and when five conferences were determined to become the "power" conferences. In many ways, this shift was unfortunate to long-term traditional and geographical rivalries.

Making a 16-team conference work—where some schools only played basketball and Olympic sports—required creativity and a strong commitment from each member school. Mike Tranghese, the Big East commissioner, was masterful at keeping things together and earned high compliments from his fellow commissioners.

This experiment—started by Dave Gavitt, the first commissioner of the Big East—of creating a new conference that had national standing and tremendous rivalries in great markets was a tremendous success. It also gave attention to a then fledgling sports network called the Entertainment and Sports Programming Network, today known as ESPN. The creation of the Big East Conference and its growth is one of the truly transcendent stories in the history of college athletics.

Ultimately, TV money caused the conference to break up. I don't believe college athletics will again experience the friendship and commitment that those ADs shared to help one another. It was a unique time and a unique conference where ADs sometimes voted against their own interest for the betterment of the conference.

The conference ADs created wonderful friendships that developed out of mutual loyalties and respect, including people like Vince Nicastro of Villanova, Jake Crouthamel of Syracuse, Jeff Long at Pitt, Ed Pastilong of West Virginia, Jean Ponsetto of DePaul, Kevin White of Notre Dame, Bob Driscoll of Providence, and Joe Lang of Georgetown, among many others. The Big East Conference office, led by the well-respected Commissioner Mike Tranghese and his deputy commissioner, John Marinatto, had great insight into the problems we faced then and were going to face in the future. Every AD benefited from their advice and leadership. All of these colleagues were people of their word.

There were interesting challenges along the way. For example, Jeff Long, then the AD at Pittsburgh and now at Kansas, worked with me to pass a conference policy that no school could accept nonqualified student athletes for admission. The vote was 14 to 2 supporting our position. Ironically, the two schools that voted no were West Virginia and Georgetown. Georgetown's explanation was that no one could tell them how to set their academic standards. The conference did.

However, as conference realignment started to take place, it became clear to me that Rutgers's vision for growing our program—more state-of-the-art training facilities and stadiums, increased alumni and fan support, national-level achievements, and championship and bowl invitations—had to include moving from the Big East to a power conference sooner rather than later.

A Final Note about the Big East

The Big East Conference was unique and provided real rivalries in football and basketball. Its geography kept expenses down. Big East football proved it could hold its own against its BCS brethren. No one could compete with Big East basketball, which is why the ACC eventually went after Pitt, Syracuse, and Boston College—it was tired of being the nation's "second best" basketball conference. It was clear to me when Boston College led the way to the ACC that others would follow.

And as the personalities changed on the football side—both presidents and ADs—their commitment to the concept of preserving and growing the Big East Conference wavered. The Big East could have become the sixth power conference and maintained elite status in both football and basketball.

Instead, everyone ran to make their own deals. West Virginia went to the Big 12, which makes no sense. The rivalries will never be the same, as the travel is a killer for the Olympic sports teams. In fact, in its first year as a member of the Big 12, West Virginia's travel costs spiked by $2 million.

ESPN could have helped more. The Big East made the network, but there too as personalities changed, loyalties became less important, and people forgot how they got where they were.

As the years go on, the money continues to carry the day. Look at the deal the NCAA made with CBS and TNT for televising March Madness. The terrific national championship game between Villanova and North Carolina in 2016 had less interest and fewer ratings because it was on TNT instead of the "over the air" network. Money trumps exposure, and this ultimately hurts everyone, especially the schools involved.

The Big East was a noble experiment that was unique and successful until a lack of leadership and the never-ending pursuit of additional money—despite what it meant to long-term and geographical rivalries—broke it up.

THE BIG TEN AND RUTGERS

Several times, Greg Schiano, Kevin MacConnell, and I discussed Rutgers's future and the conference we would strive to join if the Big East were to break up. The one that made the most sense was the Big Ten. It is composed of Association of American Universities research land-grant universities that are similar to Rutgers. Their academic partnerships and research capabilities made this conference greater than any other of the power conferences and Rutgers's best choice.

In the end, this proved to be a key reason Rutgers was selected to join the Big Ten.

Meanwhile, we quietly explored the Big Ten. Commissioner Jim Delany, who I had many interactions with through the years during my tenure at the NJSEA, was a fellow member of the NFF and College Hall of Fame Board of Directors—and a friend too. I had several exploratory conversations with him. At the same time, Greg had talks with Coach Joe Paterno at Penn State and Coach Barry Alvarez at Wisconsin. In addition, I reached out to the brother of one of the trustees at Ohio State. And I had President McCormick call Graham Spanier, Penn State's president.

These were the steps we set in motion to lay the groundwork for entry into the Big Ten. We were focused on where we wanted to go. The Big Ten made the most sense for Rutgers academically, and football opened the door for consideration. Most people do not realize that the academic advantages of affiliating with the Big Ten far outweigh the athletic program benefits.

In response to critics who believe entering the Big Ten was a mistake, I point to two things: (1) the tremendous institutional recognition that no

other conference offers and (2) the potential to be competitive in basketball and football.

Let me relate a conversation that occurred at the initial meeting of presidents and ADs when the Big East Conference realigned with Louisville,
Cincinnati, and South Florida.

The president of Cincinnati at that time (and now the president of
SUNY), Nancy Zimpher, suggested we have some academic interchange.
The then chancellor of Syracuse Nancy Cantor cut her off, saying, "You are
not at our level." This restrictive attitude would have limited the opportunities Rutgers now enjoys as a member of the Big Ten.

You don't need excessive facilities; you need first-class facilities.
Recruiting and coaching up players are the keys to success in both football
and basketball. Rutgers has shown we can be very competitive in Olympic sports. Excessive turnover in leadership at the AD position between
2008 and 2015 has contributed to some of the struggles we have witnessed
within the Rutgers program. That being said, there are four basic tenents
of leadership that I have discussed throughout this book can be used as a
guide for success:

1. Plan a leader's succession in advance. This helps solidify changes in
   place and provides continuity.
2. Always get the right people "on the bus."
3. Keep your finger on the pulse of the enterprise. While one must del-
   egate responsibilities, he or she has to stay tuned in regularly.
4. Have checks and balances in place.

One of the hallmarks of an ethical organization is cultivating open
and honest communication and resisting the temptation to "sweep things
under the rug." When I was AD at Rutgers, I always emphasized with
my staff that if anyone had a problem, they should come to me early on.
Together, we could resolve minor situations before they spiraled out of
control.

CHAPTER 8

CHOOSING COACHES AND DOING IT RIGHT

As an AD, your legacy is determined by the coaches you hire and how they run their programs. In turn, coaches must meet the objectives and measures of success their ADs expect. Their vision must be clear, and the student athlete must come first. Success for that student athlete is the responsibility of the coaches and athletic department.

To take charge of any large enterprise that is impatient for change, one must follow the steps of responsible leadership:

- Create a vision for where you want to be and a plan for getting there. Understanding this means you have to be aspirational in your approach.
- Determine priorities for the overall mission and foresee challenges you will encounter along the way.
- Mobilize others to invest in the same vision because they believe in its inherent values and are willing to take a risk.
- Create standards with which to evaluate people fairly.
- Execute the vision and take ownership of it.

I truly believed I knew how to take Rutgers athletics from being stuck in a rut to where we would compete and consistently win against the finest and toughest college sports programs in America. I just needed everyone to support the vision I created so we could put it into action.

There are outstanding New Jersey high school athletes in all sports, and so many go on to successful collegiate careers outside New Jersey. We needed to attract a majority of the best to stay home and go to Rutgers. To do that, we had to elevate our programs.

That way, high school athletes could grow excited imagining how much they could accomplish for Rutgers, themselves, their home state, and their families and friends. We needed all of New Jersey to realize they had "skin in the game."

All of this required Rutgers athletics to not only compete in Division I intercollegiate sports but also win. The Rutgers community talked about it for decades. Sadly, it seemed forever suspended—with exceptions like the 1976 NCAA men's basketball Final Four team and the women's basketball squad's 1982 AIAW basketball championship. Things seldom evolved from talking about it to doing it.

FOOTBALL

Two things were quite apparent. First, for success to be realized and sustained in Rutgers intercollegiate athletics, it absolutely had to start with the football program. That was the primary focus. Remember, this was a program that was winless and the butt of jokes throughout the state and the nation the year before I arrived.

Second, football would only get off the ground by recruiting a top-drawer head coach to lead and inspire the program and its student athletes. We needed someone who would believe it was Rutgers's destiny to succeed. Whoever was selected to lead the university into the new millennium would be a crucial hire.

Whether you agree or disagree, football defines most upper-echelon Division I athletics programs (with the exception of my alma mater, Villanova!) and creates opportunities for the other sports. My mandate when I was appointed the AD at Rutgers, from the president and the board, was simple: "Fix football." Then I had to reorganize the athletic department to make it competitive across the board.

When I started laying the foundation to rebuild the football program—practically from the ground up—plenty of people offered advice. Some of the input I asked for, and some came unsolicited. Either way, the community's response was energizing. Loyal fans of Rutgers were eager to turn a new page on athletics.

Building a far-reaching plan for a program that never had one and hiring a coach to direct it aren't that different. The coaches you hire have to reflect the values you want the program to embrace.

I knew that certain values I stood for had to be part of any business or program for which I was responsible. The dilemma all Division I sports programs face is how to balance the pressures of expectations with the desire to succeed both on and off the field. At the top of the list is academic integrity. In my opinion, it is lacking in too many programs today because the greatest emphasis is placed on winning—at any cost.

I did my best to represent a spirit of integrity with the coaches my team and I inherited and the ones we brought in. I don't believe in firing staff or coaches until I've given them a fair chance to exhibit their values with how they treat the student athletes they lead. That's the only way to evaluate whether they can succeed with the kind of program you want to run. Some situations, however, do warrant immediate change.

Among the most important individuals whose advice I respected were Rutgers president Fran Lawrence; Kevin Collins, chairman of the university's Board of Governors; Ron Giaconia, chairman of the Athletic Committee; Gene O'Hara, a former Prudential CFO and subsequent chairman of the Board of Governors; and Mark Herschhorn, at the time a new member of the Board of Governors and former Rutgers football player.

The five of us knew we had major work to accomplish in our football program. If we succeeded, it would carry over to recruiting and building winning teams with outstanding student athletes for men's and women's basketball, soccer, and lacrosse, as well as baseball and the entire roster of Olympic sports teams.

I made this very plain to both the staff and the coaches up front. I wanted to ensure they knew where I stood and what our direction was from that point on. We would succeed together by universally supporting and investing in our program. Everyone—coaches and staff—had to understand that we were all in this together.

My objective for leadership was simply creating a vision, communicating it with clarity, and then executing it. I have followed that principle everywhere I worked.

Meanwhile, football was hanging over my head. When I came to Rutgers in 1998, I had inherited Head Coach Terry Shea and had to deal with an unusual situation with him. He was named the Big East Coach of the Year with a 5–6 record our first year. I was puzzled about how he or any coach could have won that honor with a losing record. But that was because Rutgers had been 0–11 in 1997, and the five wins in 1998 represented the second-biggest turnaround in Division I football that season. But in 1999, the team reverted to its previous ways, putting up a very disappointing 1–10 record for the season.

I was feeling significant pressure to fire Terry. Coach Shea was brought in following the 1995 season by the previous administration under unique circumstances. He was from the West Coast and had played at Oregon, was head coach at San Jose State, and was the offensive coordinator at Cal-Berkeley. He also coached under Bill Walsh at Stanford. After the disappointing 1995 season, Fred Gruninger was given the direction to hire someone with head coaching experience who had won a bowl championship, and Terry was the top candidate to emerge.

But being perceived as a "California guy" in a highly competitive and unforgiving state like New Jersey can be tough. I arrived in time for the 1998 season, and Terry led Rutgers to a 5–6 record that year. I gave him my word when he was voted the Big East coach of the year that he could coach two more seasons instead of one, as his contract called for, because I felt the added commitment would help him recruit. But the improvement did not continue—the 1999 season was an embarrassment—so I set down specific criteria Terry had to meet if he wanted to keep his job. He agreed to them.

I wasn't optimistic he could reach the goals I'd set for him, but he would get a fair shot at them. Academics and recruiting were paramount. The academic state of the football program seemed to be an annual burden; every year following the fall semester, 10 to 15 students would be separated from the team for not making the grade. This had to end.

I also sensed that for a variety of reasons, Terry and his staff never fully connected with the high school coaching community in New Jersey and surrounding areas.

So early in 2000, I began looking at coaches to replace Terry Shea. I also appealed to a higher authority and prayed a 54-day Rosary Novena to find the right coach (Catholics will understand!).

While still giving Terry a second chance, I knew I had to begin searching for a new coach in the almost inevitable event we had to relieve him. First, starting that process was necessary to our long-range plans for football. If we could build a winning program, many other areas of our athletic mission would also succeed. Second, we believed in taking initiative and planning ahead. Foresight was the rule, because that's how intercollegiate athletics grow and succeed. Those that only react struggle and fail.

Several people's advice influenced my search. That summer, Fran Lawrence approved a $25,000 retainer to Chuck Neinas, former Big Eight (now Big 12) commissioner and then Executive Director of the College Football Association. Chuck was a great resource on college football coaches and still is. His son Toby was hired by now former coach Chris Ash as Director of Player Personnel (Ash was hired by Rutgers in December 2015 and fired in September of 2019).

Chuck and I met during the summer and discussed how I could integrate the kind of program I wanted—one based on practical rationale, with values and academics, so I could hire a coach with the potential to win at Rutgers.

He helped me focus my thinking and was a valuable sounding board during the search. I could call Chuck and find out what he might know about a certain coach. More than that, he knew which ones were in the hunt for a new job. Because he was a consultant and not a "search firm," he had no particular favorites, and that was important. I wanted unbiased opinions.

On November 1, 2000, Terry Shea and I met in my office. I had the unpleasant but necessary task of telling him that he was not on course to meet the goals we discussed at the beginning of the year. There were still three games left to be played after we had struggled to a 3–5 record at that point. I requested that Terry announce his resignation, effective at the end of the 2000 football season. Though I was firing him, I wanted him to officially step down with the dignity that he earned and deserved as a professional and a gentleman. Terry's son, Garrett, was a senior defensive back on the football team.

Next, I had a difficult task to carry out—have a meeting with the football team and tell them. They didn't take the news well. But the 2000 season ended with a losing 3–8 record overall, including losses in eight of the final nine games and an embarrassing 0–7 record in the Big East. It was definitely time for the team and Rutgers football to move on.

Looking back, I probably should have fired Terry after the dismal 1999 season. But I gave my word to let him try to meet my expectations. Also, I had inherited two-year contracts for all the assistants, which we would have had to honor if I had made a move in 1999.

I had been keeping an eye on several head coaching prospects during the 2000 season. Once we announced Terry Shea's resignation, I received advice and suggestions from many sources. My problem, though, was that the candidates who were seriously interested in Rutgers had neither the coaching experience nor the potential I felt they needed to turn the football program around.

Once again, there were virtually no high-powered coaches who had any interest in Rutgers. I had to find either a young head coach at a lower level or in one of the smaller conferences or an accomplished coordinator who could grow with the program. But whoever the candidate would turn out to be, he had to have the drive, desire, skill, and attention to detail necessary to accomplish the task.

I interviewed several for the position, including the offensive coordinator at Notre Dame, the defensive coordinator at Syracuse, and a former Rutgers assistant who was an assistant coach in the NFL. I also asked Gary Pinckel, then the head coach at Toledo, if he was interested. He wasn't and went on to lead Missouri to significant success.

The last coach I approached was Greg Schiano, who was the defensive coordinator at the University of Miami at the time. I called Greg on a Sunday and asked if I could fly down and talk to him about leading our football program. Both Rutgers and Miami were in the final week of the regular season. He said the only time he could do it was between 7:00 and 8:00 a.m. Tuesday morning at the Miami airport. I said one hour wasn't enough time. But we agreed to meet at the conclusion of the season in my office at the RAC.

In all probability, I could not have persuaded Greg Schiano to come to Rutgers before that time. He was the defensive coordinator for one of the most successful programs in college football, and he had just completed his second regular season there in 2000. My vision for Rutgers football was still emerging and not yet in operation.

The Miami Hurricanes had a stunning national record of bowl game victories and winning season records. Conversely, Rutgers football concluded its last two years under Terry Shea with a record of 4–18 overall, going 11–44 in his five-year tenure as head coach.

During the course of looking for a new head coach, Joe Quinlan was very helpful. He worked with me each step of the way. We established another good connection with a lawyer agent in South Carolina named Craig Kelly, who represented several coaches, including Frank Beamer, the legendary head coach at Virginia Tech.

One evening in November 2000, Joe and I were sitting in our office at 11:30 p.m. talking to Kelly when he told us Frank Beamer was going to take the North Carolina job. The move would start a carousel of coaching changes.

But we knew that everything was still in play until time ran out. The next day, Beamer decided to stay at Virginia Tech. And another candidate we had our eyes on was scheduled to interview at the University of North Carolina at Chapel Hill, Missouri, and Oklahoma State; none, however, offered him a head coaching job.

Our search continued, and Greg Schiano appeared at the top of our list because he was impressive in many ways—and not just because other candidates were eliminated.

The week before Greg and I met at Rutgers, we were in Syracuse for the final game of the 2000 season, and I interviewed George DeLeone, the defensive coordinator at Syracuse. I remember Jake Crouthamel, the Syracuse AD, telling me that DeLeone would be a tremendous hire for us. I respected Jake's opinion and valued his friendship, but I was not inspired by George. Although a very capable football coach, he just didn't seem to be the right fit.

Before Greg's interview, none of the candidates set me on fire. I just did not see the passion and the vision to lead Rutgers football into the future. I recall we sadly ranked close to the very bottom of 117 Division I programs—a discouraging place to be.

During the whole process, I convened a meeting with some of New Jersey's top high school football coaches. I wanted their input and the chance to let them know they were important to me and the process. One message I received loud and clear was that the high school coaches wanted one of their own—a "Jersey guy." My message to them was also very clear: I needed their support.

Greg Schiano arrived on Sunday. It was a dark and cold November day. After 10 minutes, he looked at me and said, "I need to know your vision for the program. I have studied and worked to become a head football coach all my life. But I don't want to make a mistake because I spent a year at Rutgers as a graduate assistant, and I know how hard it will be to fix this program."

Greg got right to the point, and that's what I wanted. Now it was my turn to answer. I laid out my vision, and I could see he was listening intently to what I described.

We spent the rest of the afternoon talking about my goals for the kind of program I wanted—one that would win games, win championships, and do it without cheating and with academics a priority. Greg is a "Jersey guy," raised in Wyckoff, and a graduate of Ramapo High School. He told me that if he were to take the job, there were three people he wanted to immediately hire: Scott Walker from Cornell to be academic advisor; Jay Butler, who was the strength coach at Dartmouth; and Dave McCune, who was an assistant trainer at Miami.

I quickly began to understand how well he had thought through what he was about to do. We had dinner with my wife, Terry. I included Terry with any serious hire I considered for her input. Then Greg agreed to meet with me again on late Monday afternoon at Panico's restaurant in downtown New Brunswick, New Jersey. He had to make a recruiting call in Brooklyn that morning.

He also asked to meet with my daughter Deidre, who was an undergraduate student at Rutgers. At the restaurant, Deidre joined us, and Greg asked her questions about student life at the university.

Afterward, Greg and I started discussing salary. Greg did not have an agent at the time. I proposed a five-year contract at $500,000 a year with a series of bonuses. He said he'd think about it and let me know on Wednesday.

I was excited about how well I thought our meetings had gone. Greg stood out from the other candidates in several ways: I felt that he had the passion and the energy I had been looking for. There was also a natural charisma about him. He had carefully considered how he wanted to approach the job and his recruiting plan if he accepted my offer, and he already knew who he wanted to hire as assistant coaches.

Greg shared my commitment to values, academics, and the holistic development of our student athletes—as well as winning. Developing young men and women to be successful in their lives is, in reality, our most important task and one that is often overlooked.

Most people think that when you interview a coach, you want to talk mainly about football—Xs and Os. I'd already talked to two men I respected about Greg's coaching abilities: Dave Wannstedt, one of the finest collegiate and pro coaches in the game of football, and Joe Paterno, one of the genuine legends of college football history in America.

Dave played in the NFL with the Green Bay Packers, was head coach of the Chicago Bears and the Miami Dolphins, and an assistant coach with Dallas, Tampa Bay, and Buffalo. At the college level, Dave was head coach at Pittsburgh and served as an assistant with three powerhouse teams: Miami, Oklahoma State, and the University of Southern California.

No one ever needed to explain Joe Paterno's place and role in building Penn State into one of the greatest American college football programs of all time.

I was aware that I would be hiring the youngest Division I coach at 34 years of age. I asked Dave about Greg's readiness. Greg had been an assistant on Wannstedt's Bears staff, coaching defensive backs, when he was in his 20s. How, I asked, would Greg be able to bridge the age gap? Dave Wannstedt did not hesitate. He told me Greg was terrific at it. As I came to know Greg, I understood why.

On Wednesday, November 29, Greg called and said he would take the job. We set a press conference for Friday morning to introduce him to the media, to the Rutgers and New Jersey community, and to the team.

I arranged to have a car pick up Greg and his family Thursday night at Newark Airport. He and his wife, Christy, would spend the night at my house, and then we would go to the press conference. Things were falling in place—at least I thought so.

Thursday evening, when Greg arrived at the airport, he called me and said he was meeting with his mother and father there. That meeting lasted over an hour, which began to make me nervous. I finally talked to Greg. He admitted, "I'm very emotional. I just left all these kids—my team at

Miami. I know how hard this job is, and I'm not sure it can be done. I'm going to the hotel to sleep for a few hours and I'll call you."

I was devastated—this was not something I had anticipated. I went up to bed and said to Terry, "I can't believe this is happening." Yet I had the peace and serenity to believe the will of God would let this all work out however it was meant to be. In my heart, I believed that Greg would decide to come to Rutgers.

Meanwhile, Greg's concerns reminded me that I might have given him an almost impossible task to accomplish. But I was determined to transform the football program, and I believed Greg Schiano was the head coach to do it.

At 6:00 a.m. on December 1, 2000, Greg called and said, "I've thought it over, and if you'll still have me, I want to be your coach." I told him to meet me at Old Queens. We would meet President Lawrence, Board of Governors chair Kevin Collins, and other board members and then go on to the press conference.

The conference announcing Greg's appointment was a resounding success. From that day forward, Greg started working 24 hours a day, 7 days a week to get the job done—and do it right.

Among many followers and fans who chimed in about the hire was Dick Vitale, the outspoken and well-known ESPN analyst and a former Rutgers assistant basketball coach. Dick left me a voice mail message, simply proclaiming, "Bobby, great hire!"

There was great interest and enthusiasm at the start, as Greg said he would recruit the "State of Rutgers"—meaning primarily New Jersey and those states that touched our borders—and talent-rich South Florida. But the early years on the field were not easy for him or me or the program; the talent level just wasn't there yet. After two seasons, our teams had won only three games. There were already grumblings around the university that maybe Greg wasn't such a wunderkind of a coach after all.

I didn't listen to any of it. I knew the day I arrived that it was going to take time for the football program to be a perennial winner in the Big East.

At Greg's introductory press conference, he said he was going to build the program on a solid foundation, without shortcuts or quick fixes. I was in for the long haul and so was Greg.

After the 2002 season, and despite a combined 3–20 record, I extended Greg's contract for two additional years because he was building the kind of foundation that was necessary for permanent success. Both recruiting and player development were beginning to show real results. We agreed we needed five years from that point in time to reach the national ranking we sought together.

I took criticism from the media, some of whom had wanted Charlie Weis, who at the time was the offensive coordinator for the New England Patriots.

Greg and I knew that in order to accomplish our goals, we needed a strong partnership between the head coach and the AD. There was too much to do and too many obstacles to address. That's how we approached our business relationship, and it worked so well.

In those early years, Greg's calmness in the locker room after a loss amazed me. The first thing he would do was boost his players' spirits. This did not mean he was calm in private. Just like me, he could not accept losing. But he said he had a duty to give his players confidence to be the best they could, and he stood by that pledge every day.

I believe that a good way to judge a coach is by how he or she handles the locker room after a tough loss, which was why I tried to be present in those postgame situations at Rutgers.

Hiring Greg Schiano was only the first step toward building a successful football program and leading Rutgers athletics out of its longtime anonymity. Rutgers who? Rutgers what?

We needed facilities that demonstrated we were a first-class Division I program even before we reached that level on the field. During those years, my vision came together with Greg Schiano's tireless efforts, plus support from the Rutgers University Foundation, including Brian Crockett and Jason Kroll. I also had terrific help from my friends in the legislature in Trenton, including Senators Dick Codey, John Bennett, and Ray Lesniak;

the late Senator Bob Littell, and the late Assemblyman Walter Kavanaugh. From all sources, my team raised $26 million.

Three members of the Rutgers Board of Governors were also outstanding allies and friends. Ron Giaconia, Gene O'Hara, and Mark Herschhorn, a former Rutgers football player, stood tall for me along the way.

Greg and I also knew that as the conference alignments began to shift, Rutgers football had to be in a position to be courted or wanted—or both—by the bigger conferences. We knew two of our strengths were our location as part of the New York metropolitan market and the school's academic reputation as a major land-grant research institution and a member of the prestigious Association of American Universities. Eventually, these were two leading factors for the Big Ten Conference's invitation to become a member.

Bob introducing New Jersey native Greg Schiano as the head coach for Rutgers football, December 2000. Greg was the youngest Division I head coach at that time.

We absolutely needed the combination of a successful football program with new and refurbished facilities. More important, the stadium's size had to be part of any serious discussion about playing in a major conference.

But more than anything else, we had to show everyone that we could win!

When it came to recruiting, there was no stone left unturned. Inspired by Finn Wentworth—CEO and COO of the YankeeNets one of the founders of the YES Network, and a true friend—we created the Knights of the Roundtable. Through funds donated by prominent New Jerseyans, alumni, and other benefactors, this commission allowed Coach Schiano to travel via helicopter and private plane to certain recruiting visits and purchase iPads for players so game plans could be readily available, to name a few examples. The Roundtable allowed us to begin competing with other schools.

Greg was a very organized and detail-oriented professional. Every player had a daily plan to review with his position coach every morning.

Coach Schiano consistently fought for the things that would make the program better. They included schedule priorities so student athletes could enroll in classes they needed around their practice obligations. He moved practice to the early morning so that team members would have afternoons and evenings for classes. He designated where players would sit on the plane and made roommate assignments when the team traveled for road games.

It was all part of teaching discipline to players, and the team as a whole, so that they could perform consistently as athletes and students. Finally, every Friday morning, he met with the academic advisors to review each student's progress.

None of the changes we asked the university to make were easy. We had to push constantly. Former dean of Rutgers College Carl Kirschner was our ally in the academic process, serving as the chairman of the Academic Review Committee, which reviewed all potential football and basketball recruits.

Kathleen Shank was also enormously helpful to us. She had been an assistant coach with the women's basketball program before becoming an academic advisor. She also knew the ins and outs of Rutgers University.

At one point, a university mandate forced me to hire a different candidate to lead the academic program. She was not my choice, and unfortunately, she failed. Then I appointed Kathleen to serve as the Director of Academic Support because she was my first choice, and she was terrific.

Equally important to us was the faculty representative selected to work with athletics. We were fortunate to finally recruit Professor Tom Stephens, who has served continuously in that role to this day. He stood for the same academic values we did and worked well with us.

Once the new program started earning winning seasons, and after our strong showing at the 2005 Insight Bowl against Arizona State, Greg Schiano quickly became one of the most closely watched head coaches in the college game.

There were two public attempts to lure him away in addition to several inquiries from topflight programs. The first was in 2006, when the University of Miami wanted to hire him as its head coach. That's when I knew it was time for us to negotiate a new contract with Greg.

At the end of the 2006 season and prior to leaving for the Texas Bowl, where the team defeated Kansas State 37–10, I met with Greg's agent, Bryan Harlan. Harlan is an outstanding and principled man. His father was the president of the Green Bay Packers, and his brother is an on-air network broadcaster to this day.

We met at the Waldorf Astoria Hotel dining room for lunch prior to the annual NFF black-tie dinner. We agreed on the elements for a new 10-year contract, including steps that approached $2 million in annual salary and bonuses.

I took the outline of the deal to show Ron Giaconia, who was the chairman of the Athletics Committee on Rutgers' Board of Governors, and Rutgers president Dick McCormick. I wanted to secure their approval on the outline of the new contract. Both men were attending the dinner, and they instantly supported our new offer to Greg by initialing the official document stating the terms of our offer.

After the 2006 season, in his sixth year, I was proud that Greg was selected by five national organizations as college football's Coach of the Year as well as given the same honor in the Big East Conference. It was a major accomplishment—one Rutgers maybe never imagined. Greg's faith in the program we built together put us on the road to realizing the joint vision we shared. Except for one dropped pass and an incorrect fumble call in the last game of the season at West Virginia, we would have been in the national hunt. We were rated in the top 10 at points during the year and were number 12 in the final Associated Press Top 25 poll.

We were undefeated at home that year and ranked in the NCAA's top 20 in nine different team statistical categories, including six top-10 rankings for defense. We were fourth in total defense, sixth in pass defense, and eighth in scoring defense. It was just a dominating year, particularly on that side of the ball. In addition, we had two All-Americans: running back Ray Rice (seventh in the Heisman Trophy voting) and defensive tackle Eric Foster.

Greg Schiano was a coach who would sleep in his office during summer camp. He would work sometimes until 2:00 or 3:00 in the morning on Tuesdays and Wednesdays during the season preparing for games. He was totally committed to achieving our goals. He always said that his primary concern was the well-being of the young men whose lives all of us trusted him to develop. He delivered everything he promised and more.

Greg was also active in a number of charitable events. For instance, he and team members participated in the annual New Jersey Special Olympics opening ceremonies. Greg was also a significant financial supporter of the vice president for enrollment Courtney McAnuff's Future Scholars Program at Rutgers.

Pat Morris, another active and supporting alumnus, worked extremely hard every year running a golf outing gala to benefit Coach Schiano's three charities, Embrace Children, Special Olympics, and Missing and Exploited

Children. Pat and his fellow alum Bob Burzichelli were extremely helpful to me "behind the scenes" in many areas. They were never ones to call attention to all they did to support the athletics program, preferring to remain in anonymity. The tailgate they ran at every home football game, which was located near the Media Entrance of Rutgers Stadium, was renowned for its hospitality and was a gathering place for friends and visitors alike.

When we went to the Texas Bowl at the conclusion of the 2006 season, Pat and Bob packed their tent and went to Houston too, ran their usual tailgate, and won the prize for the best tailgate of the bowl game.

Greg and his staff were keen evaluators of talent and uncovered many "diamonds in the rough" during his tenure. An example of this was Eric Foster, the defensive tackle from South Florida. Foster was considered a two-star recruit by the so-called experts but emerged as an All-American performer. Another example of Greg's ability to spot underrecruited talent was his discovery of the McCourty twins, Jason and Devin, who worked hard at Rutgers to become outstanding defensive backs. All three of these players went on to success in the NFL.

One of Greg's mantras as a head coach was to "recruit and develop." That's a major reason why more Rutgers players than ever before have gone on to play in the NFL. Greg and his staff also had significant success with walk-on players, including standouts Gary Brackett, Ramel Meekins, Ray Pilch, and Brandon Renkart. Brackett went on to be named captain of the Indianapolis Colts and played in two Super Bowls, while Meekins, Pilch, and Renkart all became starters during their careers at Rutgers.

I always mention one noteworthy event any time people discuss Greg Schiano's significance to Rutgers football. The University of Michigan came after Greg following the 2007 season. They made a strong effort to convince him to join them. While the push by Michigan was going on, I walked to his office on a Thursday afternoon to chat and see how he was doing. He was very emotional, and I knew he was torn between his players and the great program he built for Rutgers and an opportunity to become the head coach for one of the most storied college football programs in America.

By the way, Michigan never asked my permission to talk to Greg. But Greg always came to me immediately after other programs contacted him without my knowing it and before he made any commitments to meet with them. He said he was giving Michigan's offer serious thought. Anyone would if a school like Michigan came calling.

We talked for one hour, I gave him my views, and I suggested he leave the office and go out and make a list by himself of pros and cons. We also talked about what would happen if he left, including who on the coaching staff he would ask to go with him. I certainly wanted Greg to stay at Rutgers—at least for another few years—because the football team was making history and because of his exceptional leadership.

But I had to prepare for the possibility that he might leave us to do what he considered best for his future. We decided that Joe Susan, one of the assistant coaches at the time who has since become a successful head coach at Bucknell, would be our interim coach for the Texas Bowl game.

At 10:00 that night, I received a call from Bryan Harlan. He told me he would know in 15 minutes whether Greg would go to Michigan, but Bryan expected he would go. The moment he knew Greg's decision, he would call me. When we hung up, I called Joe Susan, who was on a recruiting trip, and told him what was happening. If Greg was leaving, I wanted to meet with Joe and the team at 7:00 the next morning.

Midnight came and went with no word from Bryan Harlan, so I phoned him and said I was going to call it a day. Then at 6:00 the next morning, I got a call from a very tired and emotional Greg, who said, "I'm staying, and I will tell the team my decision."

Other major football programs approached Greg during his time at Rutgers. But those never led to any serious discussions because he turned them away. One of the things I cherished about our relationship was that after Michigan's attempt to steal him, he said to me, "I can trust you explicitly because of the way you handled the situation and the advice you gave me." I never forgot that, and it was a measure of trust in the partnership we had that forged our success.

I was disappointed for Rutgers when he became head coach of the Tampa Bay Buccaneers, but I understood. People at Rutgers, from the university president on down, had created a perception that they didn't care whether he was there or not. In my judgment, it made it easier for Greg to take the NFL offer. This is where Rutgers failed; the university must understand that they must stand squarely behind their coaches if they want any of the sport programs to succeed.

An AD has to decide whether a coach can successfully carry out the kind of program he or she wants—and then stand behind that coach. Rutgers University is not and never will be a football factory. But it competes on the field with as much determination and pride as it does in the classroom.

Joining the Big Ten gave Rutgers first-class stature. The university now must make sure that the AD has the support and financial resources he or she needs to succeed. In New Jersey, we sometimes fail to provide that support. Then we criticize too quickly.

Men's Basketball

Men's basketball at Rutgers has been a challenge through the years for a variety of reasons, with facilities and conference affiliation at the fore. The program achieved modest success in the 1960s with an emerging coach at the helm, the late Bill Foster (Foster later went on to great achievement as the head coach at both Utah and Duke). The Scarlet Knights broke through on the national front when Tom Young took over in 1973–1974. Young guided Rutgers to its first-ever NCAA Tournament berth in 1973–1974, and the following season, he took the team to an undefeated regular season and berth in the NCAA's Final Four.

But the program fell into disarray after Young left and has never been able to regain its footing. Many point to the decision Rutgers made to stay loyal to football partners like Penn State and West Virginia, declining the invitation to join the Big East in 1978–1979 and allowing in-state rival Seton Hall to take the bid instead. Rutgers basketball was relegated to the

Atlantic 10 Conference, a tough league by most accounts but possessing nowhere near the glamour of the Big East.

Some life was injected into the program in the late 1980s and early 1990s when former Scarlet Knight backcourt star Bob Wenzel took over and guided Rutgers to two NCAA Tournament bids in his first four years. In fact, the appearance in the 1991 NCAA Tournament was the last time the Scarlet Knights attended the "big dance." Recruiting never took hold, and the program wallowed in the lower echelon in the 1990s.

In my tenure at Rutgers, the men's basketball program enjoyed pockets of success but remained a huge frustration personally. We played in the postseason five times, made five National Invitational Tournament (NIT) appearances, and had a 20-win season and an NIT Final Four appearance in 2004. We knocked off Iowa State in the semifinals behind a 35-point performance by Quincy Douby before a raucous Madison Square Garden crowd. A close loss to Michigan in the championship game did not diminish the outstanding season and rekindled some of the excitement and enthusiasm for the program that was there in the 1960s and 1970s.

During my tenure, we also scored significant wins over Top 25 programs, including Syracuse, Connecticut, Georgetown, and Villanova. There was nothing like a sold-out RAC, with our fans on top of the court and the home-crowd noise bouncing off the walls. Television commentators Jay Bilas and Bill Raftery and opposing coaches Rick Pitino and Jim Calhoun noted that the RAC was one of the toughest courts for opponents, and we played before more than 50 sellout crowds during my time at Rutgers. There was an NBA first-round draft choice in Douby, and players like sharpshooters Jerome Coleman and Ricky Shields and shot blocker extraordinaire Hamady N'Diaye captured the imaginations of the Rutgers fans.

But the RAC was also one of our toughest foes. Because of the way it was designed and constructed, expansion plans became difficult. Now standing adjacent to the RAC is the RWJ (Robert Wood Johnson) St. Barnabas Athletic Performance Center, called the APC. Both the men's and women's teams have to practice in the facility, which is open to the public during the day. There is little room for hosting and entertaining potential sponsors and corporate reps.

My team and I made some impact by upgrading the locker rooms and media facilities, but I wish we could have done more. It was just not cost-effective to expand the RAC, considering all that needed to be done to bring the football program up to speed. We worked hard to improve football at Rutgers to ensure the school's entrance into a conference like the Big Ten. Now that the Big Ten is a reality, improving the facilities is a must for Rutgers basketball to be competitive, and the current AD, Pat Hobbs, has made this a top priority. He needs the help of Rutgers Nation.

When I came to Rutgers, Kevin Bannon was the men's basketball head coach. He seemed like a good coach and recruited some talented players. I was getting to know Kevin just as I did all the head coaches—his views on athletics and academics, his vision for the program, his values about coaching, and the programs' strengths and weaknesses.

What I began to learn about Kevin's relations with his players revealed an unacceptable situation that someone had to solve. That someone would be me.

It started when I heard a story about a nude foul-shooting contest that took place at a practice during Christmas break before I started as the AD.

I called Fred Gruninger, who was the AD at the time, and asked him if he knew anything about it. Fred said no. I went to talk to Kevin about it. He made light of it and said it wasn't any big deal. I said, "Don't ever do it again—if, in fact, that's what you did."

Along the way, I became concerned about Kevin's handling of the players. One particular situation involved Rashod Kent, a senior from West Virginia. Kevin left Rashod back in New Brunswick while the team headed to Morgantown to play the Mountaineers.

The moment I heard this news, I called Kevin and asked him to explain the problem. His answer wasn't a good one. I told him that I intended to put Rashod on a plane and fly him to join the team. Then I explicitly told Kevin I wanted Rashod to start the game and to see a lot of playing time because it was at home and he was a senior. Rashod apparently had done nothing wrong, so I intervened.

That summer, I was at a Rutgers golf outing when I received a call from Joe Quinlan. He told me that one of our sophomore stars, Dahntay Jones, was going to transfer to Duke. I asked Joe to find Dahntay and bring him to my house immediately.

When he arrived, Dahntay and I talked for a long time about his situation, his feelings, and his plans. I also met with his parents. Then I scheduled a meeting with Kevin Bannon and his coaches to find out more about what was going on—why a star sophomore player wanted to transfer to another basketball program.

Around the same time, I received a call from Mike Krzyzewski (Coach K) at Duke, one of college basketball's all-time greats. He told me he normally didn't take transfers, but Dahntay really wanted to leave Rutgers and come to Duke. We spent 30 days trying to convince Dahntay Jones to stay. In the end, though, he left for Duke and was successful there and subsequently had a long professional career in the NBA.

We also lost another transfer, Todd Billet, to Virginia in 2001. This really hurt because Todd was an outstanding student athlete who hailed from New Jersey. Todd's brother, Geoff, had a great career as a guard at Rutgers from 1995 to 1999, and we were all hopeful of the success the Billet family legacy could achieve within our program. That all ended abruptly with Todd's transfer.

While attending the Big East tournament in New York City in 2001, I learned that Holy Cross had won the Patriot League. It had earned an automatic bid to the NCAA tournament. I turned to Joe Quinlan and said we now had a bigger problem: one of the student athletes involved in the nude foul shooting contest who had spoken out against Kevin now played for Holy Cross, and he was going to the tournament.

Another player who transferred out became the leading scorer for Iona and led the Gaels to the Metro Atlantic Athletic Conference (MAAC) title and a berth in the NCAA Tournament. I feared that what they knew could become public and turn into another embarrassing episode for Rutgers. Unfortunately, I was right.

At the end of that season, Kevin approached me after the Providence game. He said, "You have to help me with my relationships with my players." That's when I absolutely knew it was time for him to go.

I went to Rutgers president Fran Lawrence and said we needed to end Kevin's coaching position in spring 2001. We worked it out, and Kevin was gone. But he didn't leave easily; he fought us and sued to get the remainder of his contract.

I always thought it was unfortunate because Kevin Bannon had the potential to be a good coach—he just lacked the ability to establish good relationships with his players.

When I saw things going downhill with Kevin, I told one of his assistants, "I'm going to give you some advice. Get out of here before you're associated too closely with Kevin's problems—especially if you want to stay in college basketball." He took my advice and later became a head coach. He would periodically call me and say thank you.

My first candidate to replace Kevin Bannon was Jay Wright, a bright young coach at Hofstra University. He had been an assistant at Villanova. I called Jay and invited him to dinner at my home on a Thursday evening. Terry prepared one of her special dinners, and Jay and I talked until 2:00 in the morning. He was up front with me and said the only reason he would not come to Rutgers was if the head coach's job at Villanova opened. At that time, it wasn't vacant.

We agreed to meet on Sunday and finalize the deal—until Jay talked to some of his friends. They called Villanova's president, who summarily fired Steve Lappas, Villanova's men's basketball coach, and then offered Jay the job the next day.

University presidents might stand for the values of education and enlightenment; they are also politicians who follow their own agendas.

They can pull out the long knives just as easily as awarding degrees. Higher education is a business enterprise. People at the top play hardball, and sometimes it gets rough.

Jay came to our meeting on Sunday and told me what transpired at Villanova. He kept his word and broke the news himself rather than letting me hear it from a third party. I was disappointed, but I understood.

Jay and I have laughed about it many times—oh, so close. Look what he has accomplished at Villanova. He is one of just three coaches (along with Roy Williams and John Calipari) to win the Naismith Men's College Coach of the Year Award more than once and has won the National Championship twice in three years.

My next candidate was John Beilein, who had been successful leading the University of Richmond's program. He came to campus and to my home. When he left, Terry said, "He won't come." She was right, and I suspect it was the insight that a mother has for family relationships. John had a son going into his senior year in high school and didn't want to leave. The irony was that the following year, West Virginia was looking for a coach and called me. I suggested John Beilein. He went to West Virginia, did a terrific job there, and then moved on to Michigan before becoming the head coach of the Cleveland Cavaliers.

Ed Pastilong, the AD at West Virginia, was a good and loyal friend. My suggestion represented the strong level of mutual respect our conference ADs shared.

And to this day, John Beilein and Jay Wright remain good friends with me.

Subsequently, I received a call one morning from Lenny Robbins, a basketball writer for the New York Post. He said that Phil Martelli, head coach at Saint Joseph's University in Philadelphia, was interested in the job at Rutgers. I told Lenny that Phil would never leave, and he said, "Don't be so sure."

Joe Quinlan and I went to Yardley, Pennsylvania, that day to meet with Phil. We spent three hours together. Phil said he only needed an hour to talk to his wife and would get back to me. But there was no call four hours later, and I said to Joe, "He's not coming."

Next I called Billy Donovan, the successful head coach at the University of Florida, about his first assistant, John Pelphrey. Billy was high on John. I arranged to fly him to Newark, and we interviewed him at the Marriott Hotel near the airport. He ended up turning us down.

The fifth candidate was Gary Waters, who had been successful coaching Kent State's program and had taken the Golden Flashes to the NCAA Tournament. Basketball people gave Gary high marks. He came for an interview, and we reached an agreement.

There was one problem, though. Gary wanted all his assistants to come with him. I asked him to keep Danny Hurley, one of our assistant coaches. In response, Gary said his coaches knew how to recruit. I was in a dilemma, and I made the mistake of agreeing to Gary's terms. He did not understand, to his subsequent regret, that the Hurley family is basketball royalty in New Jersey.

Gary was a good coach who cared about his players. But to his detriment, he was too nice and did not consistently enforce the program's rules. He had strained relations with some of his players. Most of all, Gary did not develop strong enough recruiting contacts in New Jersey.

One positive memory of many I have took place on one of the team's trips to Providence. After we finished eating dinner, and because it was Dr. Martin Luther King Jr.'s birthday, Gary asked the players and me to write down what they felt was Dr. King's most significant contribution as an American leader. A fascinating discussion followed, and it is one of those vignettes in my recollection of many events that made our program unique.

Probably the highlight of Gary's tenure at Rutgers was our march to the NIT championship game in 2004. Led by high-scoring guard Quincy Douby, a future NBA first-round selection, we defeated traditional Northeast powers Temple, Villanova, and West Virginia to advance to the semifinals. A win over Iowa State in Madison Square Garden put us in the championship game against Michigan, where we fell short 62–55. Still, it was a unifying experience for Rutgers, with Scarlet Knight fans, clad in red, all taking NJ Transit trains to the Garden and descending upon the "mecca of college basketball" in droves. It was reminiscent of the 1967 run to the NIT finals, led by All-American guard Bob Lloyd, when trains had to be added to the northeast line to accommodate all the Rutgers fans.

That was the really the first time Rutgers broke through on the national stage. The Scarlet Knights were tripped up in the NIT semis by Southern Illinois, which featured a backcourt of two future NBA stars, Hall-of-Famer Walt "Clyde" Frazier and Dick Garrett. Rutgers came back to defeat Marshall in the consolation game to take third place.

At the end of Gary's fifth season, I finally called him in and said we had to make a change, and we did. Sometime later, Gary told me he should have taken my advice about Danny Hurley and recruiting.

I next turned to Freddy Hill, who was an outstanding recruiter. He believed in the values that I insisted our programs practice. Freddy was a protégé of his father, Fred Hill. His dad had great success as a coach of both college football and basketball at the Division III level and was the longtime baseball coach at Rutgers.

Freddy needed more time and direction from me, his boss. I regret that I was not available to do it. I believe he could have been very successful as the program grew because he was an outstanding recruiter. Recruiting was very difficult for two reasons: we did not have a tradition of consistent winning and our facilities were woefully inadequate compared to other Division I schools. We needed relationships with both New Jersey high school coaches and Amateur Athletic Union (AAU) programs; that's how you recruit. Freddy had the latter but couldn't overcome the lack of tradition and poor facilities.

The difficulty with luring top basketball coaches to Rutgers is that we had no traditional success other than the 1976 Final Four team. We had fallen to a second-tier A-10 Conference team in the 1980s and hadn't been to the NCAA Tournament since 1991. On top of that, I was told that we could not pay market-rate salaries for a men's basketball coach.

Women's Basketball

When I came to Rutgers, Vivian Stringer was the Head Coach of Women's Basketball. She had an outstanding coaching record.

She is a wonderful woman who overcame many obstacles in her life to reach the pinnacle of her profession.

In my second year, she was taking her third team to an NCAA Final Four and did it one more time during my term. She inspired and guided her teams to earn NCAA Tournament invitations almost every year. Vivian was also celebrated by her peers when she was named to both the Women's Basketball Hall of Fame and the Naismith Memorial Basketball Hall of Fame.

Vivian is a great coach. She demands a great deal from her players. She often had great difficulties as an administrator, which we discussed frequently because I wanted to help her be more effective in that role.

I have many great memories from her tenure during my time. Coach Vivian Stringer's clubs won 73 percent of their games (a sterling 238–90 record), leading Rutgers to its rightful place alongside perennial women's college basketball powerhouses UConn and Tennessee.

We advanced to the NCAA Tournament in 9 out of 10 seasons, and included in that brilliant stretch were two appearances in the NCAA's Final Four. Most notably there was a showdown with the Lady Vols in the 2007 championship, where we fell just short. We also appeared in the Sweet 16 and Elite Eight two times each, and there were three Big East regular season championships and a Big East Tournament title during this time.

One funny incident occurred when we won the Big East regular season at Villanova. As I congratulated the team in the locker room, player Chelsea Newton jumped up and chest-bumped me! I fell backward and Vivian gasped, but I caught myself. Chelsea has gone on to become a topflight collegiate assistant coach.

As I've said throughout my years at Rutgers and in this piece, I have a great deal of respect for Vivian and what she's accomplished. There were times when I felt she was misunderstood by the media and the public. I soon learned that she is a remarkably warm and engaging individual who established strong relationships with the vast majority of the student athletes who advanced through her program. Our relationship grew strong over the years, and I believe she has always been a strong asset for the university.

Vivian Stringer is a tremendous example for anyone—man or woman—who faces adversity. Her husband died suddenly at age 47 in her presence, on Thanksgiving Day, while she was a coach at the University of Iowa. Her daughter is severely challenged and requires 24-hour care. Yet I remember times when Vivian brought her to a game. One of my more difficult tasks was to make Vivian's life a little easier while she coached.

To understand Vivian's remarkable journey—in basketball, as a parent, as an educator, and beyond—her autobiography, *Standing Tall: A Memoir of Tragedy and Triumph* (2009), is a must read. It tells the story of ascending to the top of her profession through hard work and perseverance, overcoming challenge after challenge that would cause most to simply give up and fold. I was touched by the words she wrote in the copy of the book she gave me: "You have been there—I am fortunate to have you as my leader."

I think the highlight of my relationship with Coach Stringer was when I went to the Board of Governors and asked them to make her a $1 million coach. Some board members wanted me to start at $900,000 and negotiate. I disagreed. She deserved, I said, to be paid for what she is: a nationally respected coach. I wanted her to feel respected by Rutgers for her accomplishments and her career. The university should avoid squabbling and looking cheap about a little bit of money for one of the game's most winning and finest coaches.

During those negotiations, Dennis Coleman, a lawyer with Ropes and Gray, was Vivian's agent. I came to know and respect Dennis, and he was instrumental in brokering the deal.

Also of great help was the Reverend Soaries, Vivian's pastor, who was so instrumental in helping us resolve the Imus situation.

I have no regrets about what I did for Coach Stringer. Coming into the 2014–2015 season, she had already won 929 games in her career. She has taken Rutgers to the NCAA Tournament 14 times and has led her teams to two Final Fours and several Elite Eights. She also brought a Women's National Invitational Tournament (WNIT) championship home in 2014. Coach Stringer won her 1,000th game in November 2018, and I was proud to be present.

Olympic Sports

During my decade as the AD, Rutgers was blessed with several outstanding Olympic sport coaches. Interestingly, the first coaching change I had to make was in women's soccer. Among the candidates was Glenn Crooks, a young man I knew as a sports reporter for WMTR radio in Morristown, New Jersey, who had since gone on to a successful career as a women's soccer coach at the collegiate level. He took two struggling programs—Long Island University and St. Peter's University—and led them to the NCAA Tournament.

I was enormously impressed with his drive, knowledge, and commitment to the program and his student athletes. I hired Glenn because he reflected the values I sought. He was a great hire and a terrific coach who put up an impressive record of victories and NCAA Tournament appearances. Along the way, I also hired Mike O'Neill as an assistant women's soccer coach. He took over for Glenn and has not skipped a beat with the program, reaching new heights with an NCAA Women's Soccer Tournament Final Four appearance in 2015.

With Glenn's exceptional knowledge of the game and strategy, the women's soccer team set a 2013 program record of 11 wins at home and earned its third NCAA Tournament berth in five years. He recruited some outstanding student athletes, including Carli Lloyd. Carli, a homegrown talent from South Jersey, has won two Olympic gold medals, was honored with the Golden Ball as the Most Valuable Player in the 2015 Women's

World Cup Soccer Tournament, and was the 2015 FIFA Women's Player of the Year.

By the way, Carli scored three goals and set a World Cup record for the earliest goal ever scored after official play began. One of Lloyd's Rutgers teammates, Jonelle Filigno, also played for the Canadian women's national team in the 2012 Olympic Games.

Fred Hill Sr. was a legend as a baseball coach and won three Big East Conference championships during my tenure. Freddy was one of those unique individuals who could coach any of the three "traditional" sports (football, baseball, and basketball) and be successful at it. It's only right that the new baseball and softball complex at Rutgers is named in his honor.

I hired Jim Stagnitta as the men's lacrosse coach following his successful stint at Washington and Lee University. Under Jim's leadership, our men's lacrosse team went to the NCAA several times. Jim was named as the national coach of the year in 2004, an honor he truly deserved. I was proud of the terrific program he led.

In wrestling, John Sacchi retired after many years, and I took a chance trying to find a replacement that could make a difference. I took the unusual step of hiring a high school coach named Scott Goodale. Scott was one of the most successful high school wrestling coaches in the state.

I called him in for an interview, and during our conversation, I said I would do what was necessary to enable him to become a successful college coach. That included understanding NCAA rules and making a commitment to upgrading the wrestling program, which my team did. Scott has delivered in a big way, and the wrestling program is now nationally ranked, ascending to the top 10 for the first time ever in school history in the 2015–2016 season.

Another coach who was underpaid but outstanding was Mike Mulqueen, head of our men's cross country and indoor and outdoor track-and-field program. Mike guided and inspired his student athletes so well that they earned Rutgers' first-ever Big East Outdoor Track & Field Championship in 2005 with very limited resources and poor locker room facilities.

Bob Reasso, who for 20 years led the men's soccer program to many victories and appearances in the NCAA—including an NCAA Final Four appearance (a rare feat for a school from the Northeast)—was also respected by everyone. He was an outstanding leader. He deserved much better than to be coldly dismissed in an undignified manner by my successor.

Then there were the stalwarts like Marian Rosenwasser, who was a nationally respected women's tennis coach and a good barometer for what was happening in the department and on campus. She became a trusted advisor to me.

Maura Waters-Ballard coached both men's and women's golf and was a highly valued member of our coaching family. She was loyal to our mission and a tremendous coach.

There were many other quality Olympic sport coaches, including Pat Willis in softball, Ann Petracco in women's field hockey, Chrystal Chollet-Norton in women's gymnastics, and Roberta Anthes in women's track and field. When Pat Willis retired, I hired Jay Nelson, who served until 2018 and significantly improved that program. James Robinson was also successful for the women's cross country and track-and-field programs.

The Olympic coaches at Rutgers labored in relative obscurity. They were underpaid, usually had a cubicle for an office, and had locker rooms and facilities that were simply inadequate. Still, they were extremely important to me and to our overall program's success. They worked hard and made significant strides as we addressed together how Olympic sports in universities are eclipsed too often by the revenue sports, football and basketball.

We made other changes as necessary. I tasked Joe Quinlan with running the Olympic sports programs while I was the administrator for both football and men's and women's basketball.

As our football program became successful and continued to grow stronger from 2004 forward, the spirit and the morale in the department increased. People rooted for one another. Coaches went to other coaches for advice. I thought my last five years were a particularly successful time for us. The big difficulty was that we constantly lacked

enough money to fully support the Olympic sports the way we should
for all Division I programs.

We also broadened our life-skills program for student athletes under
Kate Hickey's direction. Important to our success was the input and support from Rutgers alumnus Peter Gibson, a very successful businessman.
The program addresses a myriad of subjects, including managing a checking account, paying bills, and establishing a budget, and it is very important for student athletes when they leave college and go out into the world.

We started mandatory training with the Rutgers SCREAM (Students
Challenging Realities and Educating against Myths) Theater. This is an
outstanding program created and performed by Rutgers University student athletes, primarily undergraduates. Educational, interactive theater
programs present important information about interpersonal violence,
such as sexual and dating assault, stalking, bullying, and harassment.

I was proud that we did a lot for our student athletes while also advertising the SCREAM Theater's value to all students.

We developed one special project that dealt directly and forcefully with
the crucial social issue of sexual assault on university campuses—specifically,
date rape.

Working with Ruth Anne Koenick, director of the Rutgers University
office dealing with sexual assault services and counseling, we obtained
a grant and produced a 30-minute film that re-created a common campus situation. It opened with a scene from one of the men's team locker
rooms after practice. Student athletes talked about going to a party that
night and said they were excited about which girls would be there. Later,
the film moved to the party and showed girls who were drunk. Then sex
followed, and one girl appeared and complained about date rape the following day. The film explained what to do and how easily things like this
happen.

Our goal was to dramatically and truthfully present the destructive
impact these events can and do have. It was a realistic depiction of what
can and does occur.

Coaches Schiano and Stringer introduced the film. I asked several students to review it to ensure it accurately portrayed what can happen. It became mandatory for all freshman athletes to watch.

I even took the film to a meeting of Big East ADs and offered them the DVD to use for their own programs. Sadly, there were no takers. My perception was that no one wanted to touch the issue. More important, the rates of reported and suspected unreported sexual assaults on college campuses have risen sharply in the last two decades. Turns out, we were ahead of our time.

One of the first meetings I attended, even before my official starting date as the AD in April 1998, was with the Student Athlete Advisory Committee (SAAC), a group composed of leaders and team members from all our varsity sports. I knew how important it was to listen to this group's concerns and valuable input.

We met regularly with the SAAC, and whatever they wanted to bring up was welcome. Each team had two representatives. This was a vital sounding board for student athletes to ask questions, discuss issues and ideas, provide feedback, plan and implement community initiatives, and support one another. One year the SAAC ran a student athlete "auction" and raised more than $1,300 for the New Jersey Special Olympics. Kate Hickey did a great job communicating with the SAAC representatives and moderating the program.

Every year before May final exams, we did something we called the "Color Games," where athletes from all our teams participated in team competitions, including tug-of-war and Ultimate Frisbee. We always ended with a barbecue that everyone enjoyed. This was an opportunity to bring athletes together and mix with one another.

We had an annual luncheon, which brought all the members of the athletic department, including administrators, coaches, and all staff—from clerical to custodial to maintenance and beyond—together. It was a way to pay tribute to all we did as a family and let every member of the department know that he or she was equally important. I was very adamant about that, and I think it contributed greatly to our success. John Ternyila (Johnny T), who performed as a DJ at the luncheon, helped create a fun and positive environment.

I was also proud of the full-time medical department we put together under the leadership of Dr. Robert Monaco. We had two excellent orthopedic surgeons on call as well as a resident psychologist who was available to address student athletes' problems, such as expanding their mental approach or discussing other serious personal issues.

Dr. Monaco was dedicated to providing the appropriate medical care for all our student athletes and worked tirelessly to make our program a model that other universities would emulate.

When we became a member of the Big Ten, other schools in the conference called Dr. Monaco to discuss our program covering physical and mental and emotional health. He had a direct command from me that no student athlete who was injured or appeared injured could go back on the field or court until that player was cleared by the doctor or trainer.

Coaches' Salaries

Determining coaches' salaries was one of the few business arrangements I did not negotiate at the NJSEA. Those decisions were made strictly among the owners, general managers, and coaches and their business agents for the professional teams that played in our stadium and our arena.

As the incoming AD for Rutgers, however, I knew that determining coaches' salaries was a highly visible responsibility of mine.

Negotiating construction plans, services, contractors, costs, and timelines for capital projects is a distinct enterprise. At the NJSEA, I worked to please millions of spectators and fans, team franchise owners, state officials, and the Board of Commissioners.

Settling coaching salaries and contracts is always an unusual undertaking. It inevitably becomes personal as much as it is about business. Like every employment arrangement, salary is an official statement about an

Bob receiving the Loyal Sons of Rutgers honor, 2009.

individual's worth and value. But it's far more open and public when the employee is the head of a sports program at a public Division I university.

As the AD, I had to address many questions: What does the market say a Division I head coach is worth for that revenue sport today? What was that coach's compensation package at his or her previous school? Did his or her teams earn winning or losing records, and what about conference titles? Does the college sports marketplace rank that coach a top prospect, or has his or her value fallen after consecutive losing seasons? If the program is on the rise, will the coaching candidates also think this could be as good a move for their career?

I considered every one of those questions when I started developing plans to raise the profile of Rutgers athletics from the back page to the front page. What really mattered was success for our revenue sports of football and basketball, followed by men's and women's soccer and lacrosse. As I mentioned earlier, the salaries of assistant coaches are critical to any sport's success, and it was a real struggle getting them to nationally competitive levels. I am not sure we're there now.

Looking back at how many winning seasons and championships the coaches and student athletes from all the teams accomplished during my decade as the AD, it is a long-standing curiosity for me why Rutgers never won a Big East Conference Championship after my departure.

They didn't until former head football coach Kyle Flood, who replaced Greg Schiano, tied for the Big East Championship his first year in the position with Greg's recruits.

I always had an open-door policy for our student athletes, and I encouraged our coaches to make themselves available whenever possible to assist their athletes. We had a few situations where we rescued some student athletes from situations that could have negatively affected them in and out of college. We didn't claim to be saviors, but we tried our best to be there and listen. When student athletes learned that the open-door policy was real, there was always a chance to help someone before it was too late.

Talking about open-door policies reminds me of how I enjoyed meeting occasionally with the dean of students and presidents of various campus groups. The athletic department also scheduled an annual dinner where we discussed different athletic and nonathletic issues that were important to Rutgers students, faculty, and administrators. It was a wonderful opportunity for me to explain what we were doing to grow Rutgers sports and the university together.

Finally, I knew when we started that top-notch recruiting programs were essential for building successful college sports teams and winning seasons at Rutgers. I was also aware that Rutgers had a reputation for allowing great recruiting programs from Ohio State, Penn State, Miami, and Virginia Tech to steal New Jersey's best high school football players away.

On the morning Rutgers officially introduced me as the new AD, I called Joe Paterno at Penn State. We talked about recruiting, and I told Joe I was erecting a fence around the state to keep Penn State and other schools away from our high school football talent. Joe laughed.

Somehow, a *New York Times* reporter mentioned that conversation in a news story about my first official press conference. A week later in the mail, Joe Paterno sent me a copy of the article with a handwritten note. It said, "Bob, remember the Berlin Wall fell too. Joe."

In my opinion, the art of choosing the right coach requires the following:

- a vision for the program that includes realistic expectations based on the facilities and budget available
- a well-defined recruiting strategy that reflects an understanding of the geographic location and culture of the school
- academic standards for the student athlete that are clearly outlined and adhered to
- standards of acceptable behavior that are defined and enforced throughout the athletic department

What has changed dramatically in the past 10 years is the power of social media. It has had a major effect on culture and has impacted coaching staffs and the recruiting process.

There is an art and science to selecting a head coach—science to collect all the facts and art to determine the appropriate interpersonal chemistry the coach needs to have with his or her team.

There was a real team and family spirit during those days in the athletic department. It was a very special time.

CHAPTER 9

PROUD, WITH
NO REGRETS

Losing your job is a traumatic experience in life. Being fired without explanation is more than shocking. It's demeaning.

I was always excited about going to work every day, and suddenly it stopped. I was denied the right to choose the time when I was ready to move on, and that made me feel helpless.

I struggled to make sense of groundless allegations about my honesty and business practices that started in the New York–New Jersey media, many due to leaks from within the university. Rutgers president Richard McCormick apparently accepted them at face value. He questioned my integrity without speaking to me about the allegations and any concerns he had.

As a member of his senior staff, I expected some measure of due process. It wasn't forthcoming.

The morning following my dismissal (December 10, 2008), I summoned staff, coaches, and athletes to the RAC and addressed them briefly as a group. Several hundred student athletes and administrative staff attended.

Presentation of the Birmingham Bowl game ball when Rutgers defeated
North Carolina State, December 29, 2008. This was Rutgers's third bowl victory and fourth straight bowl appearance.

While personally stunned by my dismissal, my priority was making sure
they understood that my most important goal was for them to continue
building on the proud foundation we had established. I expressed how
much I truly appreciated all their support. While this was not something I
wanted, it was better to happen at this stage of my career than earlier in it.

I was still their leader. I needed them as much as they needed me. When
I finished my remarks, they honored me with a standing ovation. The
football team then led a procession of staff and student athletes who each
shook my hand and gave me a hug or shed a tear.

News of my dismissal traveled quickly across the state and throughout the U.S. intercollegiate athletic community. Several gratifying gestures
were extended to me almost as fast. The Loyal Sons and Daughters of

Rutgers announced they were inducting me, as a non-Rutgers graduate, in their April 2009 ceremony. I was one of very few to receive that distinguished honor. It meant a great deal to me. I understood it represented a genuine tribute from them, and I thank them for the honor. I also thank the late Walter Lieb alumnus and former member of the Board of Trustees and Overseers, who was instrumental in the nomination.

The irony is that just prior to my unimagined dismissal, President McCormick and I worked out the terms of a new contract for me. We agreed that in 2011, we would select my successor, and I would guide the transition. President McCormick told me he had the agreement of the chairman of the Board of Governors and the chair of the board's Athletic Committee. Yet he never finalized it with me, though we exchanged emails describing the terms. Many people asked if I could explain the paradox. I couldn't.

Twice during my tenure—the first and last year—the NCAA certified that our program was in compliance. It marked the first time in Rutgers history that an operating academic and administrative program received full official accreditation under the same leadership. Wouldn't acting in compliance be a testament to honesty and ethical business practices? One would have thought so.

In the chaotic hours following my departure, I recalled one particular event that might have influenced the president's decision to dismiss me without warning.

In the late spring of 2008, an internal audit of the athletic department was leaked to the *Star Ledger*. The document, which was principally about having IT equipment, conspicuously did not include my department's responses to its findings. Then a series of articles about the audit appeared in the newspaper. Internal audits are part of business and performed routinely to make sure that systems are functioning properly. They are meant to help improve the system. It was not out of the ordinary and not exclusive to the athletic department.

Later that year, in July, the president informed me that he intended to appoint a committee to review the questions raised by the newspaper.

Al Koeppe, a New Jersey business executive and Rutgers alumnus, would serve as the chairperson. The committee requested a lot of memoranda and information. However, I soon saw how the committee failed to live up to either its promises or its efforts.

Members did not have any extensive conversations with me or members of my staff. They only interviewed me for about 90 minutes. They questioned just two of my staff, Kate Hickey and Kevin MacConnell, for less time than they spoke with me. The investigation was not thorough enough for committee members to form impartial conclusions.

It was crucial that they understood the job of a Division I AD. Yet two of the five members were absent for my interview. How could they produce a comprehensive review when a significant part of the committee did not participate?

I repeatedly stated that as the AD, members of my team and I informed the administration about all major athletic department expenditures. Whether it was the president or the vice president for finance or administrative staff overseeing the university's budget, I made sure they always knew what was going on.

Two important people involved in our department reviews were never interviewed: Greg Schiano and Terry Beachem, CFO of the athletic department. He was responsible for all communications regarding finances, budgets, and expenditures. Terry would have known about all expenditures that were made because they either were in the budget or resulted from contract terms. He also would have conveyed the process the department went through every year in reporting its budget and expenditures to the university controller and how this process changed soon after Dick McCormick arrived at Rutgers as its new president.

If any so-called "off the book" expenditures were ever incurred, Terry would have discovered and reported them—period. You can't hide these things, nor would I have ever done it.

The committee's findings and final report stated that as the AD, I did not violate any university policy or act improperly: "In entering into all

of these agreements on behalf of Rutgers University"—every aspect of
the stadium expansion design and building, contracting materials and
services, and financing—"Mr. Mulcahy was acting within the scope of
his authority, consistent with prior practices and consistent with appli-
cable laws."[1]

The report also recommended additional oversight and attention to all
athletic department operations through the office of the president and the
AD working together. I supported their recommendations.

To this day, I do not know if the newspaper stories forced the president to
respond immediately, and publicly, by holding someone responsible before
ordering a committee to objectively investigate and separate the truth from
baseless allegations. In hindsight, it seemed that's what happened.

During those days of unusual personal crisis, I vividly recall how others
acted and reacted with impressive personal grace, dignity, and profound
compassion. What they did and said was a lesson about handling difficult
situations with dignity and decency.

Jon Hanson called and took Terry and me out to dinner. He offered me
an office to rent in his building. Steve Kalafer, one of the partners of Flem-
ington Car and Truck Company, asked me to serve on the board of the
Somerset Patriots Independent Baseball League team and subsequently
as a senior advisor. Sister Rosemary Jeffries, president of Georgian Court
University, asked me to join its distinguished Board of Trustees.

Many others were welcoming and expressed their friendship to me.

I reflected proudly on several testaments of recognition to our program
during my decade of service. In 2007, the *Newark Star Ledger* published
"Rutgers, an Amazing Season," a beautiful pictorial and narrative work
about the Rutgers football team's historic year in the Big East. It included
a memorable introduction titled "You Couldn't Make This Stuff Up" by
Jerry Izenberg:

And then there's Louisville. Ah, Louisville.

The night the old guard pulled its red sweaters out of mothballs and went upstream, red team. Students who didn't even know where Rutgers Stadium was two years ago became an army—a loud army—to watch the Scarlet Knights play the third ranked Cardinals.

It was the night that best epitomizes what Schiano and Bob Mulcahy, the athletic director who took a chance on the young coach and never lost faith, did to make Rutgers the best damned college football story in America.[2]

I also appreciated a commentary by Bob Braun, the *Star Ledger's* distinguished columnist who covered education across the state for 50 years, published on December 22, 2008. Words praising my decade of leadership were heartening hours after I had been taken down. Yet two short sentences truly summarized one of *our* program's highest achievements: "There is no University of New Jersey. But there is a Rutgers football team, Jersey's team."[3]

In early fall of 2009 before the start of football season, a plaque was installed on the Scarlet Walk opposite the football statue that commemorates the birthplace of college football in the United States. It stated the same words that the Loyal Sons and Daughters used to acknowledge me as an inductee and what my staff and coaches had accomplished. It was another act of respect and kindness by them, and it meant a great deal to me.

I will always remember fondly and appreciate the support of the Rutgers fans, coaches, and staff who stood by me, our program, and our teams. They were certainly a major part of our overall success, and they remain loyal to this day.

Looking back, one of the things Rutgers lacked was a strategic athletic mission and vision. I remember when we opened the club area in the stadium. People walked in and said, "We never dreamed we could have created anything like this." It's one of those moments I will always treasure.

Dreams—they were always in abundance among my coaches and staff.

Notre Dame AD Kevin White and then president of NACDA awarding Bob
the AD of the year award for Division I, Northeast, 2007.

In 2010, the NFF paid me a great honor. I was presented with the John L.
Toner Award for Outstanding Administrative Ability as Athletic Director.
This distinguished honor placed me in the company of some of the finest
ADs in college sports. Words can't express how I felt that evening.

I remember my message the day Rutgers president Fran Lawrence introduced me to the media and university community as the new AD: "There
are many universities where academics, cultural activities, intramural recreation, and Division I athletics combine to create an extraordinarily rich,
diverse campus life. Rutgers will be at the top of that list."

Together with extraordinary coaches, staff, and student athletes, the
journey Rutgers athletics took from 1998 to 2008 propelled us to the top
of that list. We did it. Division I athletics at Rutgers became a respected
partner to academic excellence and a vibrant university-wide culture for
all students.

Was joining the Big Ten the right thing to do? I certainly think so. Could Rutgers have planned much earlier, much smarter, and far better about managing and affording all phases of athletic operations and growth? I definitely think so. I believe that joining the Big Ten was a step toward trying to define what Rutgers's role as a state university was to be in New Jersey. It showed Rutgers had the will to be visionary.

With the benefit of time and reliance on my family and faith, I now look more reflectively on a decade of success at Rutgers. I still share a bond with the entire athletic staff, and I feel pride for what we accomplished together. I will always be a Scarlet Knight.

I once asked Brendan Byrne, "Why did you hire me as chief of staff?" He said one word: "Integrity." I always remember what he said and what it meant.

There are two sides to every story. Mine is that I came to Rutgers in 1998 and left the same way a decade later—with dignity and integrity.

CHAPTER 10

AFTER RUTGERS, AND LEADING ISSUES FOR NCAA SPORTS

As Rutgers football's first season in the Big Ten was ending in 2014, Graham Couch, a reporter from the *Lansing State Journal*, called me. Rutgers was on its way to Michigan to play at Michigan State University for the first time in 10 years.

In 2004, Rutgers was still in the Big East Conference. Greg Schiano began his fourth year as head football coach. Since he took over in 2000, I had watched him work day and night to rebuild a program that, up to that point, had recorded more losses than wins. In its opening home game of the season, Rutgers defeated the Spartans 19–14 on ABC TV Sports.

More important, 2004 marked a turning point for the football program's future. It was also a defining moment for the athletic program, for students and alumni, and for Rutgers's expanding reputation on a national stage.

Even during those early and tough years of reconstruction, Greg and I never doubted or lost sight of our long-term vision. We believed we could transform the program. We were determined that Rutgers football would rise to become a respected and winning force in the top tiers of the NCAA's ranks.

Now it was 2014. Michigan State, still one of the finest college football teams in the NCAA, was hosting Rutgers, a new member of the Big Ten. This time, the Spartans came away the winner, 45–3.

Rutgers has continually suffered over what and who it wants to be. People with a long history at the school had an expression for it: Rutgers wanted to be Princeton during the week and Penn State during the weekend. After decades in obscurity, the athletic program was still trying to find its way when I arrived in 1998.

Today it can be both. Being part of the Big Ten offers Rutgers opportunities to forge important academic research partnerships with other conference schools that are renowned for their academic as much as their athletic prestige.

Isn't it ironic? Athletics carried Rutgers to center stage, the place it longed to be on a national level. Now it will play Penn State every season instead of imagining it.

Rutgers leadership has wanted to earn the acclaim of academics and athletics together as far back as the first intercollegiate football game between Rutgers and Princeton in 1869.

Unfortunately, for too many years, many senior administrators and a fair number of faculty were simply unwilling and afraid to commit both the willpower and the resources necessary to get there.

The price was investing in an athletic program that could compete against and beat some of the best intercollegiate programs in the country. Athletics finally carried Rutgers into the Big Ten. New and challenging academic partnerships will develop out of it, improving lives and societies around the globe.

Why? I believed when I arrived at Rutgers that the way to reach its mission for higher national honors and respect was to fix football. Do that, and all the other things the university wanted so much would follow. I was not alone in this assessment, as the Board of Governors mandated me to pursue such a mission.

Rutgers football has come a long way. But it still has more to accomplish if it wanted to achieve its goals.

In its Big Ten inaugural year in 2014, the football team was 3–5 in the Big Ten–East Conference. It ranked fourth after Ohio State, Michigan State, and Maryland but ahead of Michigan, Penn State, and Indiana.

Think about that—ranked ahead of Michigan and Penn State. Prior to Greg Schiano coming on board to lead the program, practically no one would have imagined Rutgers football finishing ahead of those two football dynasties.

I'd call that a pretty respectable performance by former coach Kyle Flood and his football team for a rookie season in one of the NCAA's five Division I power conferences.

Mr. Couch wrote, "Rutgers found its way to the Big Ten against incredible odds but not by accident—its football rise willed by a visionary athletic director and an undaunted coach, against a spirited but outnumbered idealistic resistance."[1]

That idealistic and stubborn resistance came and keeps coming from people like Professor William Dowling and his microscopic legion of ideologues and college sports deniers. They continue to blame me, Greg, and the revenue sports of football and basketball for corrupting Rutgers's mission to equally and effectively educate all students.

Professor Dowling still refuses to acknowledge that the vision we initiated and pursued when I was the AD has earned Rutgers sports the national respect the university sought for decades—probably as far back as the first college football game.

During my 10 years at the university, I continually searched for a proper ethos that focused evenly on academics and athletics. All my coaches shared that balanced philosophy. Meanwhile, we also understood how money's influence forced an ongoing battle with the role and the importance of academics for student athletes.

We never took for granted the priceless value of a college education and the opportunity for each of our athletes to receive one.

I knew the best way to take on Professor Dowling and his followers would be to ignore them. Sadly, being so set on his views prevented him from ever listening to or considering ours. To me, the football program's success was essential for earning a national affiliation (the Big Ten). That success could lead to more far-reaching significance and benefits to academics than athletics. Therefore, it is not athletics versus academics but athletics for academics.

THE KNIGHT COMMISSION

Since its formation in 1989, the Knight Commission has promoted advancements aimed at strengthening the "education mission of college sports."[2] Formed by the John S. and James L. Knight Foundation, the commission's initial goal was to address rising athletic scandals and low graduation rates among football and men's basketball players. Those two issues were considered threats to the American higher educational system.

Among its members are major university presidents and chancellors, the commissioner of the Big East Conference, and eminent leaders from business and journalism.

The commission published three significant reports between 1991 and 1993. Their purpose was to present a unified position from leaders in intercollegiate athletics that could direct reforms in college sports in the early part of the decade. They are as follows:

1. "Keeping Faith with the Student-Athlete: A New Model for Intercollegiate Athletics" (1991)[3]
2. "'A Solid Start': A Report on Reform of Intercollegiate Athletics" (1992)[4]
3. "A New Beginning for a New Century: Intercollegiate Athletics in the United States" (1993)[5]

While the studies were prepared in the early 1990s, when I was still running the NJSEA, the reports included a "Statement of Principles"—10 of them—that I repeated in 2001, when I was the AD at Rutgers.

Together, these wise principles represent a realistic vision for university presidents, schools, ADs, and their athletic programs to follow. Moreover, they encourage student athletes to receive a good college education and to play their sports. The following are some examples of the Knight Commission principles:

- The educational values, practices and mission of this institution determine the standards by which we conduct our intercollegiate athletics program.
- The responsibility and authority for the administration of the athletic department, including all basic policies, personnel and finances, are vested in the president.
- The welfare, health and safety of student athletes are primary concerns of athletics administration on campus. This institution will provide student athletes with the opportunity for academic experiences as close as possible to the experiences of their classmates.
- Every student athlete—male and female, majority and minority, in all sports—will receive equitable and fair treatment.
- Continuing eligibility to participate in intercollegiate sports will be based on students being able to demonstrate each academic term that they will graduate within five years of their enrolling. Students who do not pass this test will not play.
- We will conduct annual academic and fiscal audits of the athletics program. Moreover, we intend to seek NCAA certification that our athletics program complies with the principles herein. We will promptly correct any deficiencies and will conduct our athletics program in a manner worthy of this distinction.

When I was the AD, we went through the NCAA certification process twice, and both times the organization determined that we were compliant. Several departments within the university participated, including admissions, financial aid, academics, and student representatives. One challenge we faced was trying to align the athletic department's mission statement with the university's because at that time, no one could find the university's mission statement.

The "Statement of Principles" is still relevant more than 20 years later. Yet in the past several years, a groundswell of opinions about college sports running universities versus an education-first, sports-second philosophy—particularly concerning the revenue sports of football and basketball in the NCAA's Power Five conferences—has stirred controversies, and battle lines have been drawn.

The Knight Commission's work is critical. It should be a prelude for ADs, coaches, and university leadership to resolve persistent and troubling issues in college athletics at all three division levels—particularly within the Division I's 65 member universities. It will be each institution's responsibility to address them as they apply to their programs.

I will discuss some of those high-profile issues in the following section. However, I think it is important to first provide some historical context about the NCAA.

The NCAA's original purpose was to address the issue of deaths in college football. Formed in 1906 (subsequent to a meeting called by President Theodore Roosevelt), the NCAA functioned as a body that would dictate how the game of football was to be played—thus leading to the advent of the forward pass and the creation of downs, which were intended to reduce injuries. At the turn of the century, the main organized professional team sport was baseball. Professional football and basketball leagues developed in the ensuing decades of the 20th century. The NCAA expanded its purview, attempting to keep pace and coordinate with professional sports, but unfortunately, it has done so ineffectively—which brings us to our current set of circumstances.

The Issues

Athletic and academic leadership across the university system must address several specific problems confronting intercollegiate athletics today. They cannot keep ducking the issues. It is time to face them and repair the system.

If I were the next president of the NCAA or the new president of a major public university, I would form partnerships to address the following issues.

1. *Self-Government for the Power Five Conferences*

On August 7, 2014, the NCAA Board of Directors approved a monumental program that would give 65 universities in the Power Five conferences—the Big Ten, the SEC, the ACC, the Pac-12, and the Big 12—unprecedented autonomy to create and regulate their programs.

The proposed actions would give the richest five conferences nearly untouchable self-rule. Schools could grant stipends and scholarships to athletes, offer improved health insurance, and ease restrictions between players and agents—benefits that none the remaining 300 Division I sports programs could offer.

The Big 12's commissioner said universities in the power conferences needed a preemptive move to separate them from all the other schools. He mentioned that lawsuits against the NCAA were hindering the big-time programs and their operations. "Something has to give, and times are changing. We can't be as egalitarian as we have been in the past. We just can't be as generous anymore,"[6] he told the *New York Times*.

The commissioner's reference to the Power Five conferences' schools leaving the others in Division I to fend for themselves pointed to the widening breach in college sports between what's frequently called the haves and have-nots.

The NCAA board vote was 16–2 in favor of the proposal, with the presidents of Dartmouth College and the University of Delaware voting against it. Dartmouth president Philip J. Hanlon said in a statement, "I worry these changes will further escalate the arms race in college sports, which, in my opinion, is not in the best interest of intercollegiate athletics, or higher education more generally."[7] He was right.

An ongoing issue, one involving intercollegiate sports versus university leadership, begs this fundamental question: Who runs the program?

Historically, university presidents among Division I schools have been responsible for their schools' athletic programs. In the 1980s and 1990s, calls to raise huge amounts of revenue through TV contracts and bowl games from more vocal boards of governors, wealthy donors, and influential alumni has put unprecedented pressure on presidents and, of course, ADs.

Today, a university president's tenure is shorter. Boards and alumni associations are stronger and more outspoken. The responsibility for running programs falls to the AD, where tenures average 6.5 years.

Most of all, there are many more impatient, even hostile critics among trustees, alumni, deep-pocket donors, and the media who all believe they could run the athletic program better than the AD. Social media has become a convenient platform from which critics demand winning programs the moment they smell blood in the water.

What do we need for responsible self-rule by teams in the Power Five conferences?

I hope the NCAA has not burned all bridges with respect to the Power Five. I believe conference leaders must recognize their responsibility to the highest mission of their universities—that is, to fully and effectively educate student athletes to graduate and go on to lead productive lives.

I worry that the gulf in responsible leadership between the Power Five and the NCAA is already too wide. The Power Five will grow stronger while the NCAA's power will diminish. The impact of the Knight Commission's work could also weaken. Big Ten commissioner Jim Delany attempted to address some of the prevailing issues for the future. He also admitted that he didn't think his suggestions would be accepted, which is unfortunate. I would urge Jim not to give up prematurely.

I believe the changes he outlined are crucial for the future of Division I sports if it wants to retain its amateur status and academic balance, which I will elaborate on later.

2. Student Athletes and Unionization

On March 26, 2014, a regional director of the National Labor Relations Board (NLRB) ruled that Northwestern University's football players were also employees of the school and earned the right to unionize and participate in collective bargaining.

The possibility that not only Northwestern University but all private schools that play Division I sports could unionize, with student athletes becoming paid employees, marked a nearly seismic moment for college sports.

Hardly 48 hours had passed following the NLRB's announcement before the internet and social media were flooded with opinions. Some were in clear support of Division I athletes being paid; others were adamantly opposed.

I believe the NLRB's ruling was a mistake. It was political in nature. If student athletes were employees of the school, the concept of college athletics would become invalid.

I do believe student athletes should receive the full value of their scholarships, which should include a stipend that covers the full cost of attendance. Becoming employees would grant student athletes the same powers as tenured professors, who are unionized because they can bargain collectively—an advantage that other students would not have. Schools playing loose with figures that determine what a proper stipend amount should be for a student athlete in efforts to recruit him or her present another obstacle. Each school has a responsibility to monitor its conduct and its integrity.

3. Antitrust and Athletes' Rights

A federal judge handed down a significant antitrust ruling on August 8, 2014, that strongly defied the NCAA's sovereignty.

It started when Ed O'Bannon, a star player who helped lead UCLA to the 1995 NCAA Men's Basketball Championship, spotted his likeness in a video game in 2009 and was not pleased. First, no one connected with the video game—neither the creator nor the company that produced it—sought and secured his permission to use his image. Second, he never received any monetary royalty or other compensation for its use in a money-raising venture.

O'Bannon led a group of plaintiffs who took the NCAA to court—a court of law, not a basketball court. U.S. District Judge Claudia Wilken issued an injunction preventing the NCAA "from enforcing any rules or bylaws that would prohibit its member schools and conferences from offering their FBS [Football Bowl Subdivision] football or Division I basketball recruits a limited share of the revenues generated from the use of their names, images, and likenesses in addition to a full grant-in-aid."[8]

Her ruling affected Division I college football and basketball recruits entering school in 2016. Its future impact could be sizeable. It represents unprecedented support for student athletes. More than that, it is a blow to the NCAA's own longtime belief that it is impervious to any outside controls.

There are interesting conditions associated with Judge Wilken's ruling. For instance, the NCAA can

- set a cap on the amount of new compensation that FBS and Division I men's basketball players can receive while in school, which cannot be less than an athlete's cost of attending school;
- establish rules that prevent using money held in trust for student athletes to gain other financial benefits for themselves while still in school; and
- set up rules preventing universities from offering different sums of deferred money to athletes who are in the same recruiting class and on the same team.

Michael Carrier, a law professor at Rutgers Law School–Camden and an antitrust expert, made an interesting comment on the day of Judge Wilken's ruling, which was published by *USA Today*. He said, "I think for the NCAA, this is a huge loss because for the first time you have a court looking at its prized defenses, things like amateurism and competitive balance, and saying this is not persuasive. This has to be viewed as a significant win for the plaintiffs and significant loss for the NCAA."[9]

Alongside Ed O'Bannon's case is another historical student athlete exploitation lawsuit. It is particularly significant to me because Ryan Hart, the plaintiff for the class-action suit and my son-in-law, was a record-setting quarterback for the Rutgers football team from 2002 to 2006.

Ryan played in 38 games during his four years at Rutgers. He totaled 8,482 yards passing, threw 52 touchdowns, and averaged 223.2 yards passing per game.

Ryan also played a key role in my plan as the AD to reposition Rutgers higher in the ranks of Division I football. He was the quarterback who led the team to the 2005 Insight Bowl and ended the school's 27-year bowl drought.

Now, we are addressing an athlete's rights and what the law says about persons or organizations using that athlete's image. To do so without consent is commercial exploitation.

In 2009, Ryan filed a lawsuit against Electronic Arts (EA) for violating his right to publicity. The lawsuit stated that EA misused his likeness in an NCAA video game it produced and sold.

His likeness in the game was not just vaguely similar; it was exact in several ways. The animated quarterback had Ryan Hart's skin and hair color, his height and weight, and the number 13 he wore on his Rutgers football jersey. It showed the same helmet visor he had. The left wristband Ryan wore during games was visible in the video game. Even the video's player biographical and career statistics were included. They were Ryan Hart's bio and career stats.

The video game did not give players' names, but it did not have to. Ryan and anyone who played with him, coached him, or followed Rutgers football knew the likeness was his, not some fictional character.

EA thought Ryan's lawsuit would not hold up in court. On November 12, 2010, it filed a motion for the court to dismiss his case or a motion for summary judgment as an alternate avenue to fight him. What was EA's reason? The court should find in its favor because the company was exercising its First Amendment rights in using his likeness.

Ryan Hart's legal counsel said, "Not so fast." Discovery in the case was still outstanding, and any summary judgment would be premature.

The federal district court announced its decision. Stating that Ryan Hart failed to demonstrate how discovery would enable a decision for the plaintiff, the court granted a summary judgment for EA.

However, one of the strengths of our legal system is that plaintiffs or defendants can appeal an initially unfavorable judgment by the court. That's just what Ryan Hart did, and he sought due process.

On May 21, 2013, in a 2–1 decision, the U.S. Court of Appeals for the Third Circuit in Philadelphia overturned the lower court's ruling. "The digital Ryan Hart does what the actual Ryan Hart did while at Rutgers: He plays college football, in digital recreations of college football stadiums, filled with all the trappings of a college football game," said Judge Joseph Greenaway. "This is not transformative; the various digitized sights and sounds in the video game do not alter or transform the appellant's identity in a significant way."[10]

EA's position that a First Amendment shield allowed the company to use the former college quarterback's likeness did not hold up. The video game maker failed to demonstrate it had transformed Ryan Hart's identity to a significant degree.

Judge Thomas Ambro, the single dissent, wrote that the majority penalized EA for "the realism and financial success" of its NCAA football franchise.[11] He was referring to the NCAA's licensing operation.

EA and other companies like it pay the Collegiate Licensing Company to use school and team names, uniforms, and fight songs in video games. "E.A.'s use of real-life likeness as 'characters' in its NCAA football video game should be as protected as portrayals (fiction and nonfiction) of individuals in movies and books," the judge wrote.[12] I agree.

However, the other two judges said the lower court was wrong. In their majority opinion, EA did not meet legal tests used to determine whether an individual's right of publicity should win out over any First Amendment protections.

EA failed to meet the transformative use test. Ryan Hart's animated video character was much closer to a celebrity's "likeness" than the creator's "expression" of it.

Also, under the predominant use test, the U.S. Court of Appeals said EA's video game did not have any First Amendment protection.

The appellate reversal of the lower court ruling meant that Ryan could attempt to collect some of the profits EA received from its 2004, 2005, and 2006 sales of the video game.

Still, these two major antitrust rulings have significantly diminished the NCAA's level of influence and control over athletes' lives and futures. For too many years, the NCAA's difficulties in settling lawsuits have significantly reduced its influence. By creating the Power Five conferences, some felt that the NCAA abdicated its legal duties. Their inability to work out issues and go to court was an influence for establishing the power conferences.

I propose that when a student athlete's image or likeness is used for monetary gain by a third party, the marketing firm and the university should jointly develop a formula to determine a fair-value amount of compensation for the athlete. In addition, any financial benefits gained from using an athlete's likeness should be placed in a trust for him or her to receive following graduation or the expiration of his or her eligibility.

I never offered counsel or interceded in Ryan's lawsuit; only followed its progress.

Ryan Hart and Ed O'Bannon stepped up to fight for the rights of former and current student athletes. They pursued legal action on behalf of others as much as they protected themselves.

Their cases were about principle rather than money because they will not receive much in compensation. Yet because of Ryan's challenge, he and others represented in the plaintiff's action could be compensated in the future.

This historic court case personifies the NCAA's arrogance. It is stubborn and refuses to settle lawsuits like this. The case should never have come to this point. The NCAA should have represented the best interests of student athletes rather than unrestricted and unregulated commercial gain. Now it is paying the price.

4. Academic and Athletic Scandal

The NCAA and the athletic community preach the values of playing sports, yet we send mixed messages. Governing boards, university presidents, and ADs who not-so-subtly tell coaches that winning is everything undermine the highest tenets of athletics. There are consequences for academics too.

In 2014, the University of North Carolina (UNC) was embroiled in a dramatic academic scandal. It involved athletes from the revenue sports of football and basketball. The longer the story played out, the more disgraceful the scandal grew.

Football and basketball players were taking "paper" or "no show" classes held almost entirely in the school's African American Studies Department. All they had to do was maybe turn in one paper. *Maybe* is the operative word there—maybe they turned in a paper or they didn't, and maybe it was written by the student athlete or it wasn't. University records revealed that the department chairman and his secretary orchestrated the scheme by creating a shadow curriculum for student athletes.

The story grew worse. UNC was further disgraced when an official investigation led by Kenneth Wainstein, an attorney and former Department of Justice official, revealed that phony classes went on for as long as 18 years so that student athletes could continue playing. The scandal grew when evidence indicated that more than 3,000 athletes and nonathletes took fake classes.

As the investigation progressed, the story of Mary Willingham, the university's former academic advisor for athletes, came to light. Ms. Willingham first grew troubled soon after arriving at the school in 2003. She noticed that many athletes were educationally unequipped to do college-level work. Her 2005 research indicated that out of the 183 football and basketball players she investigated, 60 percent read between the fourth- and eighth-grade levels, and 8 to 10 percent read below the third-grade level.

Ms. Willingham was concerned by the trends she saw and talked to a local newspaper reporter in Raleigh. When her account was published, UNC became the lead story on network TV and page one in national newspapers.

Almost instantly, sources from different camps of the UNC community accused Ms. Willingham of being a whistle-blower and airing the university's dirty linen in public. Then things suddenly changed for her.

She received an integrity award from the Drake Group, which advocates reforms in college athletics. At the same time, UNC, which always gave Willingham exceptional performance reviews for her job in the past, started a campaign to discredit her. She received her first negative review, and school officials ordered her to sit in a basement office doing clerical work. Mary Willingham left her position under pressure on May 7, 2014.

A central point to this continuing NCAA issue is a statement Ms. Willingham made soon after leaving UNC: "If universities are going to continue to admit students who aren't ready to do the work, the NCAA should pay for 15 months remediation, after which the athlete would have to pass a test."[13]

What happened at UNC highlights the ongoing challenge to ensure that student athletes get an excellent college education—one of genuine value—while the revenue sports of football and basketball often consume up to 40 hours a week of a student athlete's time. This is a nonstop priority for college and university ADs across the country—not only four-year institutions but also two-year community colleges.

Unfortunately, the NCAA and UNC found a loophole that allowed UNC to escape punishment. In my view, the university should have been severely penalized. Yet schools like UNC that tie themselves closely to the AAU earn a favored-nation status, allowing them to avoid any penalties.

There is no excuse for what happened at UNC or at Syracuse University.

On March 6, 2015, the NCAA issued a 94-page report that summarized investigations covering an eight-year period. Investigators found that Syracuse University's athletic department and men's basketball program had committed violations for more than a decade. Among the infractions reported were forged classwork, basketball players receiving cash payments for appearances at volunteer events, and an almost complete disregard for the school's drug policy.

The NCAA imposed tough sanctions. It vacated 100 men's basketball victories under longtime Syracuse head coach Jim Boeheim, and the team lost 12 scholarships over the following four years.

Respect for academics begins with the university president and the AD. It must involve all the coaches and the academic support staff serving all the programs. This should be an unchangeable rule for all sports. Scandals involving student athletes and academic programs have become the norm rather than the exception across Division I programs. They also happen, although rarely, among Olympic sport athletes.

ADs, head coaches, and the athletic-academic support staff should share and review information on student athletes' academics on a weekly basis.

When I started at Rutgers, the football program had academic support set up in two converted concession stands off the concourse of the stadium. My team and I revamped that system. I appreciated how all the head coaches working under me took this responsibility seriously.

Greg Schiano set up his own program for the football team. Every Friday morning, he met with either or both of his two academic support advisors, Scott Walker and Kathleen Shank. They discussed academic issues happening with the players. I also met regularly with the academic support professionals because I cared a great deal about academic success for all our athletes.

I agree with the views Bo Ryan, the respected former head coach of men's basketball at the University of Wisconsin, expressed following the 2015 Final Four national championship game. He shared his thoughts in a postgame press conference after his Wisconsin Badgers played so well versus a great Duke team, only to lose to the Blue Devils in the final minutes.

Ryan talked about the importance of connecting athletics and academics for his players. He talked about his program's successful strategy of finding and developing "local talent" in Wisconsin and then enabling those student athletes to pursue a four-year program of excellence in both athletics and academics.

He politely yet firmly said that Wisconsin basketball does not subscribe to the "one and done" philosophy—when a player leaves his or her institution after one year to move on to the professional level—that is fostered at the University of Kentucky under head coach John Calipari. Of course, Ryan would be proud for his players to be drafted by the NBA and have great pro careers if that's what they wanted. But he also promised his players that they would graduate with degrees from academic programs that would prepare them for successful and productive lives without basketball.

I criticize the NBA's leadership, including Rutgers graduate and former NBA commissioner David Stern, for failing to take a position similar regarding the NFL. The NFL requires three completed years of academic studies before a college athlete is eligible to turn professional. In my view, it is another instance where power and money—rather than the student's best interests—influence people's judgments, decisions, and actions.

I realize that in basketball, an athlete's development happens quicker in most cases than a football player's development. Yet I still would like to see the NBA require student athletes to complete at least two years of college before they can enter the draft.

We will still see exceptional athletes who can bypass the entire college system, although I think it is their loss. It would be better for the student athlete to earn some solid university-level academic accomplishment before entering the pros.

By staying in school for at least two years—even better, by finishing four and graduating—the revenue sport student athlete will have learned how to communicate, reason, make critical decisions, and develop relationships that will serve them well for the rest of their lives.

My position on this is reinforced by Coach Mike Krzyzewski's approach to building the "Redeem Team" as he describes in his book *The Gold Standard*.[14] Perhaps the most successful active college basketball coach realized that most of the players on the national team had either not attended college or left college early. He recognized that they were missing the opportunities that are afforded by the college experience; therefore, he organized activities that replicated those opportunities. As it turns out, his formula was the key to our renewed success on the world stage.

Universities must often determine how to attend to student athletes who come poorly prepared by inadequate primary and secondary public school systems. I strongly recommend that colleges and universities offer remedial courses for student athletes in those situations so they can develop the skills they need to succeed in college and later in adult life.

Some key elements are required to attain respectable academic performance in intercollegiate revenue sports. First, you have to create a strong academic support staff. Second, you need coaches who believe in academic success and will enforce the system by limiting playing time following poor performance in the classroom. One thing athletes understand is playing time. In my view, it is leverage coaches can use to ensure performance.

Coach Schiano held morning practices so his players could choose from a broader range of courses offered on campus. This allowed them more opportunities to enroll in classes and majors they wanted but could not take because of conflicts with football practice and training schedules. Scheduling was a priority and a continuous issue for us. It took several years to work things out with the Rutgers administration.

We made every effort to ensure that our student athletes understood why getting a college education was important. We wanted them to realize that their sport was something they did, not who they were.

The national statistics on how few intercollegiate revenue sport athletes make it to the professional ranks proved our point. Research published in 2015 by the NFF and College Football Hall of Fame shows the following:

- 772 colleges and universities field football teams at all levels (FBS, BCS, Division II, Division III, NAIA, etc.)
- 70,000 college football players are listed on their rosters
- 0.5 percent of those made NFL opening-week rosters in 2014
- 3.3 years is the average NFL player's career
- 6 years is the average time period for a college student to obtain a bachelor's degree

Between 3 and 6 years is not enough time to call anything complete and finished, particularly for someone who hasn't yet reached 30 years of age.

Making an NFL or NBA roster does not guarantee lifelong financial and personal success either. In 2009, Sports Illustrated estimated that 78 percent of NFL players were bankrupt or dealing with significant financial stress within two years of ending their careers. It also reported that 66 percent of NBA players were broke within five years of leaving professional basketball.

Being bankrupt and being broke are not the same conditions. In addition, multiple factors can contribute to an individual's financial ruin.

Too often, the hiring process for coaches is done for one reason only: to win. The efforts to ensure that coaches run a well-rounded program that really does educate student athletes in the classroom and later in life has, in my opinion, become convenient lip service. The bonuses for academic achievement, including graduation rates, should be significantly higher.

Collegiate athletic leaders have a responsibility to provide a strong life-skills program so these athletes can be productive throughout their lives.

5. Lessons from Penn State

The NCAA Executive Committee's decision to impose stiff sanctions against Penn State University athletics following the child sexual abuse scandal in 2011 was reversed in 2014.

The decision to roll back the sanctions was an action almost unheard of in NCAA history. It took a firestorm of public criticism that rose up quickly to question the NCAA's traditionally unchallenged rule of law.

In July 2012, the NCAA imposed a set of severe punishments against Penn State because of the sordid child sexual abuse scandal involving its longtime former defensive football coach, Jerry Sandusky.

Though the NCAA stopped short of completely shutting down Penn State's program, the penalties seemed almost cruel in scope. There were 10 scholarships lost per year for four years. The number of scholarship players on the football team was capped at 65 compared to the traditional 85, and this restriction was also in place for four years starting in 2014.

The university was also forced to remove all of its victories from 1998 to 2011, which meant that legendary coach Joe Paterno would no longer be the all-time leader among his peers in wins earned coaching college football. Finally, Penn State was put on probation for five years.

Across social media and from their letters to elected officials in Washington, the enormous Penn State University family at home and abroad said that it wouldn't let the NCAA's harsh actions stand. Exacting criminal punishment is not under the purview of the NCAA but rather under the jurisdiction of the criminal justice system. While there were problems with reporting lines at Penn State, the student athletes themselves should not have been penalized.

It took almost three years for the NCAA to acknowledge that it did not have lifetime privileges to judge, punish, or reward intercollegiate athletic programs with impunity.

Some saw the decision as a dramatic step away from the organization's long-standing iron rule and toward a more contemporary response influenced by public and social opinions.

I believe that Mark Emmert, NCAA president, using emergency powers to sanction Penn State, presented a clear example of the NCAA usurping its authority and punishing the wrong people—and hurting its credibility.

Student athletes had nothing to do with the Jerry Sandusky affair, but they were the ones penalized. Later on, the NCAA reduced some of the original sanctions.

It would have been far better for the NCAA to sit down with Penn State and work out a program that did not punish the wrong people. The Pennsylvania attorney general's office should have investigated criminal actions and enforce penalties—not the NCAA. The real effort has to be sincere intentions and actions that address sexual violence in our society.

6. Head Trauma and Concussions, Student Athlete Health and Safety, and the NCAA

"The most important finding is that college football players are intentionally playing through the vast majority of potential concussions," said Chris Nowinski, cofounder of the Sports Legacy Institute, a concussion education group.[15] He was referring to a 2013 study conducted by researchers at Harvard University and Boston University.

The research team found that (1) college football players reported having 6 suspected concussions and as many as 21 "dings" for each single concussion that was diagnosed and (2) offensive linemen were the least talkative about any head injuries and symptoms with team trainers and other personnel.

Offensive linemen experienced diagnosed concussions and assumed concussions at a ratio of 32:1. They experienced the highest rates of suspected concussions and dings among all player positions.

Nowinski and Christine Baugh, a Harvard researcher and the study's lead author, published their findings in the *Journal of Neurotrauma*. Their research sample was 730 Football Championship Series players representing 10 universities in seven states.

An important concussion-related lawsuit filed against the NCAA by four former college athletes was settled in July 2014. The settlement required the NCAA to change its guidelines for managing concussions as well as provide $75 million for medical monitoring and research.

The lawsuit, which originated in 2011, accused the NCAA of negligence for waiting until 2010 to adopt a formal concussion policy. And when it finally did, said the plaintiffs, the organization still did not set any minimum policy standards.

"Continuing to turn a blind eye and continuing to essentially pretend that the concussion isn't as severe as it is, those are the things we say make the NCAA negligent," said Joseph Siprut.[16] Mr. Siprut was a Chicago-based attorney representing the four former athletes: two football players, a soccer player, and a hockey player.

In their lawsuit, the former athletes charged the NCAA with the following acts of irresponsibility:

- not properly educating competitors about the dangers of concussions
- not creating all-inclusive policies to diagnose and treat head injuries
- failing to draft rules establishing minimum guidelines to follow when a student athlete who suffers a head injury is unable to return to competition

Under the settlement's terms, the NCAA would require member schools to review and update their policies concerning concussion-related injuries. It would also compel them to institute improved return-to-play procedures.

At the time of the agreement, the NCAA only required schools to have concussion management plans on file. But it never recommended what steps the plans should include nor imposed any penalties when institutions did not follow their own guidelines.

Also important, the settlement set up a 50-year medical monitoring program for several million current and former NCAA athletes in any sport. Of the total settlement, $70 million would be marked for screening to monitor long-term damage, and $5 million would cover research.

Interestingly, the settlement did not include any monetary damages for the four plaintiffs or other former athletes who were part of the original lawsuit. However, it did allow the plaintiffs and other athletes to file separate personal injury lawsuits.

On January 22–23, 2014, the NCAA and the College Athletic Trainers' Society cosponsored the Safety in College Football Summit. A large working group of experts from related areas of intercollegiate sports and medicine addressed three primary issues involving high-contact sports, particularly football:

1. Independent medical care in the collegiate setting
2. Concussion diagnosis and management
3. Football practice contact

Participants reviewed evidence-based data and agreed that there was scant research material on the underlying effects of limiting contact in football practices.

A majority expressed support for the NCAA to create a project with the U.S. Department of Defense aimed at conducting a clinical study to define the natural history of concussions.

Following presentations and discussions, participants agreed it was necessary to prepare summary points supporting independent medical care in the collegiate setting, concussion diagnosis, and managing football practice contact.

The summit group produced an initial consensus statement for participants to review and comment on before becoming association policy. Additional statements developed in 2014 established guidelines for (1) improved student athlete safety, (2) year-round football practice contact, and (3) independent medical care.

Meanwhile, the NCAA still faces criticism for the way it handles concussions and head trauma. Critics say it lacks stronger oversight and is reactive rather than proactive.

For example, in conversations with the national media, NCAA officials suggested that health and safety should be under the direction of member schools. The organization also suggested that universities should frequently monitor their policies and protocols concerning head trauma—not the NCAA.

Of course, institutions need protocols to guide their decisions and actions in all areas of university life. But administrations also need to enforce them because they are responsible to the students, their most important constituents.

Ultimately, in my view, the athletic department, the AD, and the medical staff must determine which student athletes can resume playing and when.

In a statement to CNN, the organization said, "NCAA enforcement staff is responsible for overseeing academic and amateurism issues. They do not have the authority to make legal and medical judgments about negligence."[17]

The NCAA's critics believe it has done too little in past years to deal with concussions and return-to-play studies.

In 2003, the NCAA partly funded two studies that found that athletes need a full week to recover from a concussion, and players who sustain one concussion are more likely to have another.

You cannot have a one-size-fits-all standard because each individual case is different. If a player suffers a concussion, he or she should abstain not only from practice but possibly from classes as well. The cognitive function of the brain needs rest—it's that serious.

This is especially critical because college-age students are more susceptible to second-impact syndrome, which occurs when a player suffers a subsequent concussion when he or she has not sufficiently recovered from an earlier concussion. The consequences of that subsequent concussion are typically more severe and possibly even life-threatening.

In the meantime, seven years passed before the association spoke more assertively about concussions. Yet in 2010, it issued only guidelines rather than rules for best practices. This left room for critics to wonder whether the NCAA's commitment to reducing concussion injuries in football and other high-contact sports was genuine or merely posturing.

"The NCAA does have a problem," said Dr. Robert Cantu, a Massachusetts neurosurgeon and a prominent researcher on sports head injuries in
the United States. His research has indicated that concussions are scien-
tifically known to hasten the onset of memory impairment, Alzheimer's
disease, depression, and suicide. "I'm very disappointed that they didn't
proactively put in place best practices for management of concussion
when they knew what really should be done."[18]

At the same time, the NCAA's 2014 consensus statement on concussion
guidelines laid out a four-phase plan to address the following:

1. Education
2. Preparticipation assessment (a brain injury/concussion history;
   symptom evaluation; cognitive assessment; and balance evaluation)
3. Recognition and diagnosis of concussions
4. Postconcussion management

The plan also outlined substantial guidelines for players' return to
activity, return to play, stepwise progression, and return to academics.

I believe the NFL and NCAA have a responsibility to fund responsible
and ongoing research involving all forms of head trauma and other injuries that are common in organized sports. At the college level, that has to
include baseball, lacrosse, soccer, wrestling, and other sports. This issue
needs more immediate attention followed by rule changes.

One example in football would be a rule change eliminating the traditional kickoff, where violent collisions occur, and starting play with the
ball on the 25-yard line. Another opportunity would be to review and better determine what the rules say about offensive and defensive linemen's
stances.

The goal would be to lessen the impact of straight-ahead hits and
contact at the line of scrimmage. Leaders of youth, high school, and college football need to have a real discussion about this issue and make a
determination. We're talking about changes that don't affect the value of
the game.

Reducing and preventing rates of head trauma and improving health and safety for student athletes requires dedicated research, financial support, and leadership coming from the NCAA, university administrators, ADs, and the sports medicine community.

Despite guidelines and studies from recognized organizations, each school has a responsibility to make sure that doctors rather than coaches determine when a student athlete can and cannot return to the field. Despite all other controls that may exist, each school must be responsible for every one of its student athletes.

It isn't necessary to do away with organized football in American life. But we have a crucial and immediate responsibility to review the way we play the game. Most of all, we want to ensure that retired and former college and professional athletes suffer far less from chronic and debilitating trauma and other life-inhibiting injuries later in life.

Growing national awareness and concern about concussions and head trauma should not be limited to intercollegiate programs and college-level athletes. Rates of athletic concussions and chronic orthopedic injuries affecting primary and secondary school athletes in soccer, cheerleading, football, lacrosse, and baseball have risen significantly in recent years.

Girls from preteen through teenage years who play soccer experience higher rates of concussions, ACL tears, and hip injuries than boys do. It isn't uncommon for adolescent girls playing soccer at high levels of competition to suffer multiple ACL tears before they reach 17 years of age.

Young athletes also represent the majority of ulnar collateral ligament reconstructions, or Tommy John surgeries, in the United States. Findings from research sponsored by the American Orthopaedic Society for Sports Medicine at its summer 2015 conference indicated national rates of young athletes having Tommy John surgery rising at 9 percent annually.

Teenagers 15 to 19 years old represented nearly 57 percent of all Tommy John surgeries between 2007 and 2011. Brandon Erickson of Rush University Medical Center in Chicago proposed that having this procedure early in young athletes' careers will improve their chances of receiving a college scholarship to play baseball or being drafted to a professional team. But he thinks they are undergoing serious surgery with unrealistic expectations. Just 1 in 200 boys playing high school baseball is drafted to play Major League Baseball. The study also reported that athletes who had surgery before reaching college had a higher risk of suffering another injury when playing at the college level.[19]

In addition, passionate parents who want their kids to play well enough to earn a scholarship put way too much pressure on the child to perform at levels that their still-growing bodies are simply not ready to sustain. Moreover, playing on competitive travel squads raises the chances for children to suffer serious injuries, including head trauma and chronic orthopedic conditions.

Leaders in college athletics across the United States from all three divisions must ensure that their programs provide and enforce the right protocols to prevent and treat all forms of head trauma.

Finally, we must provide leadership that will better manage conditions that can allow young people to compete too intensely and too early in their physical development. To emphasize again my firm position on this, universities; their ADs and coaches; senior administrators, including the president and provost; and medical personnel must keep their word by setting protocols in motion as the highest priority and then hold their staff accountable.

Money's Influence on College Sports

The pressures of finances, TV revenues, and huge salaries paid to professional athletes have created an unrealistic environment affecting student athletes. It is increasingly difficult for athletics and academics to compete on equal footing, particularly among the 65 schools that compose the Power Five conferences. Universities and ADs are under constant pressure from the media, trustees, and donors to produce winning programs at the expense of student athletes' academic achievement.

After two years as the head coach at Rutgers, Greg Schiano had won three games. Yet I extended his contract for another two years. I believed he needed an additional five years to build the foundation for a program that would invest in athletic and academic success for the team and for our student athletes.

I took a considerable amount of criticism from the media and fans. Some suggested I should have hired Charlie Weis, former head coach at Notre Dame and Kansas, instead of Greg. I took heat for hiring a defensive coach instead of another team's head coach to lead Rutgers football into the future.

The critics were wrong. Greg developed a phenomenal football program. It was the program that thousands of alumni, administrators, faculty, supporters, and influential people across the state had prayed for. It had finally arrived, and Rutgers thrived as a premier football enterprise.

Now they had that team, and Greg was the perfect coach for Rutgers for its time. He was outstanding as our head football coach and took the program forward. He met and then surpassed everyone's expectations.

Greg was a disciplined individual. He held everyone connected with the team, and especially himself, accountable on and off the field. He brought toughness and national respect to the program. Especially important to the football program was having a head coach with a real vision. Greg had started to envision success even before he arrived.

Now part of the Big Ten, Rutgers's senior administration and athletic leadership will have to join other universities and come to terms with several debated issues in college sports.

Today, revenue sports and the universities that support them—*and* those schools that are financially dependent on them—can be allies or enemies on any given day.

Division I football and basketball programs in and beyond the Power Five conferences have turned into subcultures within academia. They create total loyalty and hardline opposition among competing internal factions. Presidents, boosters, boards of governors, alumni, faculty, students,

ADs, foundations, and even elected officials with ties to the schools choose sides. They can't live with each other or without each other.

Football programs at most Division I schools in the Power Five conferences have significantly more money thanks to lucrative TV contracts. Rutgers has to wait several years to cash in on TV revenues since it joined the Big Ten.

Meanwhile, the school operates with a huge financial deficit, missing millions in annual state appropriations to higher education that it has not received for nearly a decade. But athletics represents less than 3 percent of the university budget.

Rutgers isn't alone; it stands in line with hundreds of other public state universities operating in the red.

I agree with others who point out that the gulf between the haves and have-nots in college sports is growing too fast. Revenues do not come anywhere close to covering expenses. The quest for money tends to speak louder than reasonable judgment and common sense would dictate.

This is a worrisome trend. Then again, maybe it isn't. That depends on whom you ask—a Division I football coach with supporters writing checks for his program faster than the school can cash them or a Division II women's lacrosse coach who can barely afford mouth guards and face masks for her players. "Those five-year-old game day uniforms will just have to make it through two more seasons," she'd say and feel helpless to do anything about it.

The growth of Division I revenue sports, lifted by huge sums of money, is simultaneously exciting and scary. It creates feelings of unbridled power that is addicting and dangerous to a university's health.

During my 10 years at Rutgers, I constantly worked on building a better, more responsible intercollegiate athletics system. Today, the pressure to succeed and win at any cost is too prevalent. Conferences are breaking up. The Power Five are growing stronger while the NCAA grows weaker, which leads to less cooperation.

I knew that building a winning football program was linked directly to raising a university's national standing, increasing its enrollment, raising school spirit, and expanding many areas of development and alumni support. All would benefit from a stronger financial base.

Given my experience as an "insider," I've earned the right to raise concerns about the very culture I participated in, even if my role is smaller now. If the relationship between academics and athletics in America isn't severed yet, it is badly fractured in several places.

Everyone seems worried about enrollment. Some believe bigger football and basketball programs are the answer because they are often looked on by students as enhancements for campus life in general.

As a case in point, the University of Alabama at Birmingham eliminated their football program but then quickly reinstated it to enhance student life. Hence they will protect revenue sports if it means bringing in more male students. While female students outnumber male students, this demographic fact was not historically anticipated, and administrations are seeking to increase the number of males who enroll. There are those among academia's senior ranks who are willing to forsake necessary improvements to infrastructure and adjunct faculty pay.

Division I athletic programs compete aggressively for authority as much as money. Trust and cooperation among leaders are dissolving. I am sorry to say, but it is now "every man for himself."

In the next decade, two things could happen: the Power Five conferences could overtake the lesser ones and then run them like corporate subsidiaries or we might see conferences operate as independent for-profit federations with like-minded missions that are totally disconnected from higher education. The for-profit path would carry with it significant tax implications.

From where I used to work, there is a disturbing erosion of cooperation among ADs. Money and power have driven a wedge between those who used to negotiate schedules and broker deals where everybody won—their programs, student athletes, academics, school morale, enrollments, fundraising, alumni relations, and healthier financial support.

Pressure to win significantly affects how an AD creates his or her non-conference schedule, with traditional rivalries falling by the wayside. For example, I always thought Rutgers basketball should play all the major New Jersey schools rather than only a couple of them.

I believe that a severe breakdown in interdependent institutional controls—in some cases, outright abdication—underlies this rising dysfunction and distrust in America's intercollegiate athletics.

The system may be broken, but it can be repaired and rebuilt to be even stronger. First, boards of governors, university presidents, and ADs must work together for the long-term health and growth of their institutions rather than their personal agendas. We also need to restore openness, ethics, and sound principles of leadership.

Power and money could be shared more equitably for everyone's benefit. Professors and ADs could cease bickering over who's more important to the school's future. Academics and sports each could earn national honors and national championships.

University presidents could stand up like responsible heads of state instead of hiding in the corner anytime athletic boosters or academic department chairs start calling them out.

Money has the potential to destroy the integrity—even the morality—of intercollegiate sports as much as it could enrich the system. Reform should begin with a more level-headed system for sharing money across all three divisions.

So now the question becomes, Who is the first to step up and fix it? The NCAA is certainly not capable in its current form of solving this problem. All educational institutions bear the responsibility for the health and welfare of their students. As Dr. Ken Reed said, this is what could force the government to step up and legislate issues related to intercollegiate sports.

A Report by the Big Ten Conference Commissioner

Jim Delany has served as the Big Ten Conference's fifth commissioner for more than 25 years. He has worked in the trenches, designed the architecture, managed the infrastructure, and developed the vision and mission for virtually every major project in intercollegiate athletics. In July 2015, a panel of 12 persons working in college sports and organized by CBS Sports named Jim the most influential person in college sports.

I have known and worked with Jim for as many years as he's impressively forged breakthrough initiatives in college athletics. He is a remarkable man with vast leadership experience. When he offers suggestions about the life of college sports, you can be sure that those ideas were generated by his substantial insight. There are many fine individuals working at the highest levels of intercollegiate athletics; Jim Delany is a preeminent personality among his peers.

In February 2015, Jim wrote a groundbreaking 12-page letter titled "Education First, Athletics Second: The Time for a National Discussion Is upon Us."[20] It delivers a persuasive message. Jim suggests that freshmen student athletes should be ineligible to compete. He sees this as a realistic attempt to address the longtime gross imbalance favoring athletics over academic performance—specifically among college football and men's basketball players.

Jim uses forceful, frank words in his important dispatch to appeal to influential people throughout higher education and intercollegiate athletics:

> If we could send a reasonable yet unmistakable signal that intercollegiate athletics prioritizes education over athletics, why would we not do so? If we could clearly distinguish the collegiate model from the professional model by illuminating two clear paths—an educational path and a professional path—particularly for athletes who have high expectations of playing their sports professionally, should we not do so?

We are at a critical moment in the evolution of intercollegiate athletics. Regardless of attendance, television ratings, or any other manner
in which football and men's basketball may be thriving, if the educational experience for football and men's basketball student-athletes is
not healthy, then those sports are not healthy.

If we cannot defend the educational value of the student-athlete
experience in the sports of football and men's basketball, then we cannot defend the model as educational; if we cannot defend the model as
educational, then we cannot defend the model.[21]

Jim recommends changing the model for the revenue sports in higher
education. His letter addresses national opinions, including criticism from
across the country, even in some regional strongholds where college football and basketball are almost worshiped as holy institutions.

He writes, "Central to much of the criticism is the notion, particularly
in the sports of football and men's basketball, that the purported educational mission of intercollegiate athletics is a façade—that the true mission is to make money off the efforts of players who 'get nothing' and serve
as minor leagues for the NFL and NBA."[22]

Reading his landmark letter, I instantly recognized the qualities that
have earned Jim enormous respect year after year from admirers and
skeptics across the college sports community in America. You can always
count on him to address genuine issues and offer constructive alternatives,
truthfully describe problematic conditions affecting college sports, present
open-minded viewpoints supported by accurate information, and defend
the virtues and values of college sports while pointing out their flaws.

He addresses several key concerns about college football and men's basketball becoming more important than academic performance for student
athletes in both the Big Ten Conference and many of the other 65 schools
in the Power Five conferences.

First, inequalities between revenue sport athletics and academic performance largely affect student athletes of color who entered college with

lower academic qualifications for admission than other undergraduate students. Jim declares, "If we cannot defend—through an examination of actions as opposed to words—that education is the paramount factor in our decision-making process, then the enterprise stands as a house of cards."[23]

Second, the college sports community in America should celebrate important achievements made in recent years: (1) core course requirements for initial eligibility leading to graduation within five years of enrollment have risen and (2) increasing graduation rates tied to improved sports teams' APRs reflect a commitment to education. Yet Jim Delany writes,

> There are, without a doubt, examples of exceptional students who have also excelled at the highest levels of college football and basketball. On the whole, however, there is evidence to suggest that there is an imbalance between the "student" side and "athlete" side of the "student-athlete" equation, with the "athlete" side carrying the day.
>
> Football and men's basketball student-athletes have remarkably high expectations that they will be able to compete professionally, they spend more time on their sports than student-athletes in other sports, yet in a variety of academic metrics, they lag behind all other sports—not by a little but by a lot.
>
> Consequently, we have no choice but to view the individuals and teams that are academic high achievers not as the norm but as outliers. Further, we have no choice but to worry about the health of the educational experience (i.e., the "student" side of the equation) in those two sports.[24]

Early in his letter, Jim emphasizes that there is "immense goodness in the enterprise of intercollegiate athletics."[25] The enterprise offers many opportunities for young people with athletic talent to attend college and graduate.

He continues to say, and I believe correctly, that if not for their athletic abilities, these students probably would not attend college. That's often the way it happens with the revenue sports.

Commissioner Delany cites research showing that as many as 20 percent of student athletes across all the NCAA sports are first-generation college students. Being able to graduate from college for those students could enhance their lives beyond the playing field and college.

Third, both anecdotal and factual evidence shows that athletics, not education and academic achievement, dominate the four- and five-year experiences of student athletes in football and men's basketball more than ever before.

Male student athletes competing in the revenue sports are shortchanged by the system. Three examples stand out:

1. Former UCLA basketball player Ed O'Bannon's landmark case against the NCAA for allowing a private multimedia company to sell video games using his unauthorized image for financial gain.

2. The nationally disgraceful 18-year history of academic malfeasance at the University of North Carolina involving revenue sports student athletes described earlier in this chapter.

3. Early 2015 efforts by Northwestern University football players to form a union and participate in collective bargaining to protect their right to share in the lucrative earnings football earns for the university. They also stated in federal court that as student athletes at Northwestern, academics were clearly far less important than playing football.

It is also disconcerting that many football and men's basketball players at the Division I level do not seem to mind being convenient pawns to further sports as the focal point of college and not academic achievement. Too many student athletes have their sights set on going to the pros right out of college or being drafted before graduation.

Few of them—and I mean few—stand any chance of making it to the big game (those statistics I cited earlier). More unsettling is that many people with enough influence and power to correct this dangerous assumption do not or will not raise their voices in protest on behalf of the priceless quality of earning a college education.

My point is that revenue sport student athletes who consciously ignore knowledge and skills that will prepare them for life after the NFL and the NBA—if they even make it—are naive. They are making a big mistake.

Finally, another major concern Jim raises is whether revenue sport student athletes view athletics as far more significant to their college experience than academic accomplishment. The amount of time each week that college football and men's basketball players spend practicing, training, and playing their sports indicates that academics suffers in the process. Sports have the upper hand.

The principal recommendation Jim makes in his report is to explore "a year of readiness"—specifically, a freshman student athlete in football and men's basketball would not be eligible to compete.

In this proposed system, student athletes will have a choice: they can sit out a year or pass up attending college and explore ways to pursue a desired vocation in professional football or basketball. The commissioner writes, "It is not the responsibility of intercollegiate athletics to serve as professional minor leagues in any sport."[26] The year of readiness, he says, "would allow student-athletes to have a year of assimilation to campus life before worrying about competition and the pressures and scrutiny that would follow. It would provide an opportunity for these individuals to be students before being asked to compete."[27]

I don't subscribe to a year off because it won't happen in today's world. But I subscribe to making the process right for the student athlete. A restructuring of remediation to ensure that these athletes are prepared is what needs to happen. When student athletes sit out from competition, they typically lose their edge.

Jim's recommendations urge us to be conscious of lessons learned while seeking the best outcomes in intercollegiate competition—when our teams win and when they lose.

I've never known Jim Delany to shy away from controversial issues in college sports. Not when he knew the time was right to consider changes within the system. I'm sure Jim expected some backlash from some quarters in higher education and college sports. There was lukewarm enthusiasm and barely any support.

USA Today sports columnist Dan Wolken suspects that Delany's plan will not likely see the light of day in the college sports world. It presents a radical change from the status quo. Some Big Ten coaches are skeptical, and others outwardly scorn the idea.

However, Wolken writes, the plan presents some convincing points that college coaches and administrators would be mistaken to dismiss outright: "There are inherent factors that drive toward a higher probability of academic fraud, which should be eliminated if possible."[28]

No one can deny one irrefutable fact: football and men's basketball players begin college much less prepared to be academically successful than both their classmates competing in Olympic sports programs and the general undergraduate student population.

Here are some of my last thoughts on football's role in scholastic and intercollegiate sports:

- Football is America's game. We have to make sure we fix it before it wrecks itself.
- Football represents an opportunity to many student athletes, particularly those coming from urban areas, as a way out and up.
- Football's traditions as well as its attributes should be reinforced regularly.
- This is a critical time for high school football. Parents are concerned about injuries. We have to make youth football safer as well. I suggest that tackle football should not be allowed before age 14. They should play flag football instead.

CHAPTER 11

A CALL FOR VALUES
AND FINAL THOUGHTS

[The American football contest] is a highly organized commercial enterprise. The athletes who take part in it have come through years of training; they are commanded by professional coaches; little if any personal initiative of ordinary play is left to the player. The great matches are highly profitable enterprises.

—Henry Pritchett, President of the Carnegie Foundation
for the Advancement of Teaching

When was this statement made? If you said 1929, you are correct because it appears in a report issued by the Carnegie Foundation for the Advancement of Teaching.[1] The bulletin also addressed "the use of aggressive recruiting tactics, the widespread existence of 'slush funds' and subsidies to athletes, often by alumni boosters."[2] It's time to revisit the mission of our responsibility to student athletes.

In this book, I have argued that governing boards, administrators, and ADs must possess the requisite courage to agree upon and stand by the values set forth for their athletic programs, regardless of team records. Every AD has two solemn responsibilities. First is to establish a culture where their student athletes will always be able to practice, train, and play safely.

Second is to provide the opportunity for student athletes to receive an education with skills that will support them in society and throughout life.

As the "front porch" of a university, intercollegiate athletics can be a source of building community and instituting cultural change as well as a vehicle that tests the mettle of our *better* selves. At Rutgers, my team and I envisioned possibilities and executed the plans to realize a brighter future.

As I have shared my own experiences and cited the assessments of others, we are at a critical juncture where we must reclaim and restore decency to the endeavor. During my 10 years since leaving Rutgers, I have spent much time reading about, discussing, and contemplating the state of college athletics and the challenges ahead. To this end, I am offering alternative approaches and their concomitant advantages and disadvantages.

It is the responsibility of so many working in intercollegiate athletics to safeguard and strengthen the games we all cherish. From governing boards to university presidents and from ADs to coaches and staff, all must provide leadership, daily oversight, and guidance.

We need to protect the welfare and enhance the experience of our student athletes in *all sports* while acknowledging the following:

- A strong academic experience, which includes necessary life skills lessons, should be the top priority of all intercollegiate athletics programs.
- Student athletes' physical, emotional, and spiritual health on the practice courts and playing fields is paramount and must be protected and enhanced.
- Student athletes need to be assimilated into the larger university population at our colleges, not isolated in athletics.

At Rutgers, we strove to help our student athletes reach great heights in their sport and in the classroom. We wanted them to be role models that the overall student body could look up to and of whom alumni would be proud. One tangible goal was to have the cumulative GPA of our student athletes match or exceed that of the general student body. As I often point out, 99 percent of student athletes will not have a professional career playing their respective sport; therefore, it is the university's responsibility to provide the tools and support to ensure that students receive a degree and begin their professional careers upon graduation.

When I began at Rutgers, we were playing catch-up. The student athletes had been regularly separated from their programs due to poor showings in the classroom. After a decade of hard work, the department's GPA did closely match that of the overall student body. I felt it was imperative that we publish our team's aggregate GPAs in the annual report.

We also encouraged significant community service as a tool to help develop the "whole person" and so student athletes could understand the privilege and responsibility that come with their role at a university. Participation in the New Jersey Special Olympics and the legendary Rutgers Dance Marathon (to raise funds to fight cancer), visits to local hospitals, and trips to elementary and middle schools on "Read Across America Day" are just some examples of the noble efforts made by our student athletes.

Yes, there were some behavioral missteps by a small portion of our athletes along the way, but we had little tolerance for such transgressions, something that needs to be the norm rather than the exception in all intercollegiate athletics programs. We directed and expected our coaches and staff to instill a sense of responsibility—to do things "the right way"—in our student athletes. When missteps happen, punishment should be swift and appropriate.

It's inarguable that intercollegiate athletics occupies an important place in the university, albeit not the only important place. A successful athletic program can be a centerpiece for the spirit and morale of a university.

Athletics also needs to be far more than just "entertainment for the masses," including alumni, influential donors, television executives, and marketing strategists. A delicate situation has evolved between the Power Five conferences and the NCAA that will take careful leadership and thoughtful responses to navigate successfully.

STUDENT ATHLETES, DIVISION I SPORTS,
AND THE COLOR OF MONEY

This leads to addressing the fundamental question: What is the definition of a student athlete in today's world of Division I football and basketball?

Many revenue sport college athletes are overconfident that they will move on to the pros. Unfortunately, only a very small number will succeed at the professional level, and most will have a short career. Some will be financially broke long before they approach 40 years of age. In the HBO documentary *Student Athlete* (2019), the following statistics are relevant to today: during the 2016–2017 academic year, 91,775 men played NCAA football and basketball, only 330 of whom were drafted by the NFL or the NBA in 2017.[3] These numbers further illustrate how imperative it is to provide student athletes with life skills and an education.

What should be done and who's responsible?

I think intercollegiate athletic leadership has to accept responsibility. Unfortunately, I don't believe the NCAA is equipped to address these pressing issues. The Power Five conferences have the broad influence and power to bring about change. If those institutions ignore their duty, I don't expect much will happen.

I read the NCAA's April 2017 report on college basketball and the several recommendations contained therein. I do not foresee that the NCAA will do much to address the challenges because the issues run deep, and resolving them would require revamping their business model. Since money is the driving force, no one wants to interfere with the entities that are profiting; AAU leagues and apparel companies are at the top of the list. Sadly, I don't think the courage exists to make the bold changes that are necessary.

Let's start with the student athlete. Students participate in sports as an avocation, balancing their academic, athletic, and social experiences. *Except* that this is no longer the reality for Division I football and basketball players.

In my opinion, the basketball practice of "one and done" makes a mockery of the NCAA's mission statement regarding student athletes. By following the three-year requirement, football and baseball come closest to providing athletes with a launching pad after college. In those three years, and if the institution is committed, athletes can get an academic education and improve their basic skills.

Unfortunately, intercollegiate basketball has become the minor league for the NBA. In a telephone conversation with former NBA commissioner David Stern, he showed no inclination to want to change the rules. I hope Commissioner Silver has a greater understanding of the issue.

Basketball is hostage to further corruption by the growth of the AAU leagues, their summer leagues, and the financial structure provided by the big shoe companies. As an unfortunate consequence of this system, high school coaches are losing influence to mentor and guide young players.

Athletic shoe companies operate inside college sports without any sensible controls. I don't believe anyone or any entity has the courage to fix the situation—let alone even try. Instead, the players become pawns in a much bigger money game.

Major athletic apparel brands sponsor college basketball programs and run the three major AAU circuits. When the FBI unveiled their expansive investigation in September 2017, it was alleged that executives at Adidas were bribing players to attend Adidas-sponsored schools and eventually sign with the brand once they reached the NBA. At the AAU showcases, coaches, recruiters, agents, and players interact with each other—a clear NCAA violation. The FBI report also revealed coaches arranging payments involving Adidas, a money runner, and an AAU coach. They had a single ulterior motive: ensure each player continued on Adidas's path.

How can this be fixed? There is no one-size-fits-all solution here because of the issues that need to be addressed—with conviction. They encompass the power of the AAU, the power of the apparel companies, the influence of television money, and the impact of sports agents. Yet no one will stand up to these influencers, including boards of trustees and ADs.

Why would a university bite the hand that feeds their athletic department and notoriety? We are dealing with a hypocritical, broken system. We call them student athletes, yet they are pawns in a joint financial and business environment.

The AAU has taken the role of high school basketball coaches. AAU representatives have become the agents for young athletes, showering them with money and apparel and imbuing them with a sense of entitlement. The college coach today looks to the AAU coach as the conduit for recruiting.

In April 2018, Keith Sergeant, a prominent sports journalist with NJ Advance Media, researched and posted two significant financial studies. He reported on (1) Big Ten football programs that made and spent the most money[4] and (2) Rutgers's spending on men's basketball and how it ranked in the Big Ten.[5] Sergeant's reporting reveals the enormous sums of money spent and lost relative to revenue in Big Ten football and men's basketball.

Some schools do a better job trying to educate students and provide them with stronger academic support programs. It is still up to the coach and AD to demand that students dedicate equal attention to studies and the game. If the student athlete refuses, there should be consequences. Less playing time is one option.

I think that when universities recruit student athletes, the schools have a responsibility to provide them with every opportunity to receive a fine education—both in the classroom and in life. Fortunately, we see many of the schools now offering life-skills programs.

We might also consider allowing student athletes to retain registered agents to represent them fairly and honestly, realizing that it might not cut out much of the nonsense that involves shoe companies and money runners unless there are strict controls in place. It's also worth considering creating a trust fund for players when for-profit businesses, sports and nonsports related, use them to endorse products and services.

There are many who believe that colleges and universities should pay student athletes. Although I believe in setting up trust funds with payments for students' postcollege careers—encompassing endorsement opportunities, use of likeness, sale of jerseys, and public appearances—I do not wholly subscribe to paying student athletes as if they were employees. Here are some questions that have to be resolved if we were to pay student athletes:

1. Will the NFL and NBA step up and be the financial source of funding for these salaries?
2. Will there be salary caps?
3. How do we achieve parity between schools?
4. Do we take football and basketball out of the equation and make them professional sports? If so, how do we address compliance with Title IX such that we protect the expanded opportunities for women and restore men's Olympic sports opportunities?
5. Are the athlete salaries to be taxable, tax deferred, or tax exempt?
6. Do we require a base salary that increases for every year in college?
7. Do we offer a college education as a perk of the job?
8. Do we guarantee tuition remission for a set number of years subsequent to "graduation year" of the athlete's incoming class?

This would be a daunting task and take years to accomplish—not to mention that this is not in any university's mission statement that I am aware of.

On a higher plane, we have a responsibility to student athletes that Jim Delany spoke about with conviction in his report. The Big Ten commissioner's 2015 report "Education First, Athletics Second" is a fine example of a proportional response, as is Jim's recommendation for "a year of readiness."[6] Freshman student athletes in football and basketball would be ineligible to compete because the primary purpose of attending college is to get an education. While I endorse the need to emphasize education, I am skeptical that in this day and age, a year of readiness would be a practical solution.

We can start to transfer power away from groups that exploit student athletes and return it to the conferences and schools—if there is a will to run Division I revenue sports with integrity, not with tainted agendas. This requires strong presidential leadership, strong conference leadership, and buy-in by presidents, boards of trustees, and ADs.

One option is to have the NCAA form a suborganization to oversee player development programs for basketball. The organization would take control out of the hands of the AAU because the AAU would ultimately report to the NCAA and only allow coaches to attend. Another possibility is for a group to form with the NCAA to revamp its core values. To align its mission with student athletes' expectations, schools must provide student athletes with opportunities to achieve a first-rate education and success in competitive athletics.

In many cases, the present rules are antiquated—even petty and unfair. As a flagrant example, the NCAA found a convenient loophole that allowed them not to punish North Carolina after the school was caught committing 19 years of academic fraud. Who would take this seriously if the NCAA, the ruling body, does not and will not? Once again, the system chooses to follow the money. Why would the NCAA touch a cash cow like North Carolina, which brings fame to college basketball?

The "cost of attendance" phenomenon could, and I think will, significantly alter intercollegiate athletics as we know it. We need to ensure that key decisions made by the university, the AD, and the student athlete are not influenced entirely by money.

It's time to stand up, debate the issues, and come up with real solutions that will benefit our student athletes and our institutions. We should thoroughly examine the current realities of intercollegiate athletics.

I realized the degree to which money overcomes tradition and common sense when I participated in a small committee organized by Randy Levine, president of the Yankees, and Mark Holtzman, executive director for special events of the Yankees, to move the Army-Navy Game to Yankee Stadium in commemoration of the 20th anniversary of 9/11. The proposal included the Corps of Cadets marching down the Canyon of Heroes and laying a commemorative wreath at the 9/11 Memorial and hosting a gala on the *Intrepid*. Instead, both schools decided it would be better to have the game at MetLife Stadium, where they could fill more seats and thus make more money. It was a missed opportunity for two of this country's most esteemed institutions.

POWER WITHOUT CONTROLS

I am concerned that America's intercollegiate athletic enterprise believes its own power is absolute and untainted. It teaches student athletes playing revenue sports to worship at the altar of money, gifts, and complete self-indulgence. I am uncomfortable with how much unrestrained power the college sports complex has developed in recent decades. It is contemptuous of anyone who questions its ideology and methods. If suffers from narcissism so deep that it refuses to acknowledge its defects.

Student athletes playing Division I revenue sports on full scholarship are still immature.

They are enamored of the privileges of victory, and they have developed a sense of entitlement from coaches, scouts, alumni, recruiters, and fawning patrons.

Simply look at Baylor University and its football program. The head coach failed to address sexual assault allegations against his players. He ignored the victims' accusations and accounts that incriminated players. The chancellor resigned for willfully shrugging his shoulders for years at female students' charges of sexual assault committed by football players. In my opinion, neither the players nor the head coach nor the chancellor demonstrated any apparent shame. Football ruled.

Some sports apparel companies try to exploit student athletes. They shower them with more unnecessary clothing than nonprofit foundations in the United States could ever find to clothe millions of poor and desperate men, women, and children.

My experiences at the top levels of government, business, and college athletics have taught me an important lesson about leadership: good leaders address difficult challenges by developing proportional responses and seeking collaborative solutions. The AD wants to raise $30 million to build a new indoor sports complex for men's and women's basketball? Okay. How about joining the medical school and starting a capital campaign to finance the sports complex *and* a new center for biopharmaceutical research? How about building two teams—one to reach the Final Four and another with students who could discover a breakthrough for treating multiple sclerosis, muscular dystrophy, or cerebral palsy?

The pervasive problems in men's basketball have developed over time without any credible challenge to address them. What started with free shoes, some spending money, gifts, and locking high school coaches out has spiraled out of control—now it's unethical and sometimes illegal profiteering, unchecked power by certain groups' interests, rising corruption, and money's unconscionable influence.

There are no easy or simple remedies at hand for men's basketball. But the problems are not beyond our reach—not yet. I think there are moments when one could compare Division I men's basketball to climate change and the earth's rising seas. We must begin with realistic targets to slow down, stop, and reverse the damage done before it becomes irreversible. We must begin this process now.

Values and Accountability Matter

We cannot be afraid to make bold decisions that ensure universities will maintain and cherish the intrinsic values of intercollegiate athletics. If not, we risk a variety of consequences, including investigations by government agencies that could result in legislative intervention.

The Knight Commission presented important guidelines for values in the 1990s. We need a remodeled version of that now. The culture of intercollegiate sports in America today has changed dramatically since the Carnegie report made 90 years ago. Some changes have improved and advanced intercollegiate athletics; others have created troubling issues and reversed years of hard-fought progress harkening back to 1929.

For example, a disturbing trend has developed in which coaches who are under intense pressure to win allow injured players to return to the game too soon. Coaches who are unable to decide between protecting an athlete's well-being and winning should not determine any athlete's physical, emotional, mental, and long-term fate. That goes for ADs too. Only board-certified physicians should decide when any athlete is ready to return to play.

An example of malfeasance committed by university officials, with fatal consequences to a student athlete, occurred at the University of Maryland in 2018. As I was submitting this manuscript, the University System of Maryland Board of Regents completed its investigation of the school's football program, led by then head coach D. J. Durkin. The investigation opened with the tragic and avoidable death of a player, Jordan McNair, during spring practice. By fall 2018, Washington, DC, metro news reports described a physically and psychologically abusive culture in which a strength and conditioning coach operated unchecked, with callous indifference for the safety of the student athletes on Maryland's team.

On October 30, 2018, the regents restored Durkin as the head coach—against the apparent objections of the university president. The regents' majority decision resulted in nearly instant public outrage from students, faculty, the governor of Maryland, state lawmakers, and members of Maryland's congressional delegation. One day later, the president fired Durkin without advising the board.

From the day of the football player's death until Durkin's firing, actions of the board and the university president represented an indefensible failure to live up to their fiduciary responsibilities. Unfortunately, based on my experience, most boards do not have a real sense of the athletic department other than wanting wins and pacifying its alumni base.

The irresponsible manner in which the University of Maryland conducted its investigation was disastrous for its national reputation. The Big Ten Network reported on allegations that university officials did not want to fire Durkin because the athletic department's depleted budget would force the school to pay the balance on his multiyear contract salary. That rumor circulated at the same time as news reports on the football program's repressive environment. It also raised important questions about the ability of other universities to meet the challenges facing them in Division I football and basketball.

Then there are the excessive advertising rates during March Madness that keep rising every season. In his 2015 book *How We Can Save Sports: A Game Plan*, Dr. Ken Reed addresses the issues of winning and profiting at all costs and how ego and greed drive astounding sums of money that can corrupt the system.[7]

One solution he proposes is an integrated sports policy for the country. While I understand his views, I don't think we need government intervention that will bring with it more layers of bureaucracy. However, we do need our leaders at the collegiate level to stand up for the values these great American games have taught so many people in our history.

I hope when that assembly of professionals finally convenes—ideally, sooner rather than later—it will include serious-minded university presidents, ADs, and student athletes representing all three divisions as well as community colleges.

LONG-TERM LEADERSHIP

Time is of the essence. Neglecting to review and enhance athletic administrators' responsibilities for educating these student athletes is a dangerous practice to follow.

These and other suggestions mentioned in articles and books such as Dr. Reed's on the current environment in college sports tend to agree on one major point. They warn that very little constructive progress will happen unless there is strong leadership present to support and enforce it.

I certainly advocate that position—as long as the individuals in charge can demonstrate that they have successfully managed other projects related to improving educational and life experiences for young people.

In addition, I propose that colleges and universities should establish internal committees to manage institutional controls and their effectiveness for their athletics programs. Membership would be university presidents, ADs, chairpersons of the Athletic Committee for the Board of Governors, and four student athletes—two revenue sport and two Olympic sport. It's my version of the CIA: a committee on intercollegiate athletics.

Their job will be to ensure that institutional systems effectively support the following:

- all areas of athletic operations
- student athlete academics and graduation
- conference relations
- fund-raising and development
- facilities management
- strategic planning

Some Division I programs are fixated on building college athletic centers with bowling alleys, pitch-and-putt courses, and luxurious entertainment centers just to recruit high school prospects. Hugely expensive facilities loaded with superficial attractions might please some alumni loyal to athletics, but overall, they demonstrate how we have gone to the extreme.

Academic and athletic officials should openly debate all parts of the Delany report. They should create programs that provide remedial education in math, reading, and writing skills for student athletes who desperately need them.

I stand by preserving the values of all intercollegiate sports, including the Olympic sports. The two main revenue sports, football and basketball, present some of the finest opportunities and some of the biggest disappointments for academic and athletic achievement by student athletes.

We have the ability to do this right. The central question is, When will we finally do it? Can we chart a course that requires academics and athletics to support one another?

I sincerely believe that major conversations and real plans to guide college football's current and future directions must include organizations such as the NFF. Archie Manning, the Pro Football Hall of Fame quarterback and original all-time playmaker for the New Orleans Saints, is a dynamic chairman. Archie and his very experienced colleague Steve Hatchell, president and CEO of the NFF and College Hall of Fame, along with their board members, are dedicated to achieving the mission that is stated on their website: "To promote and develop the power of amateur football in developing the qualities of leadership, sportsmanship, competitive zeal and the drive for academic excellence in America's young people."

Their national program, Football Matters, is a realistic attempt to make people aware of the value of intercollegiate football at all levels. Their local chapters have 12,000 members across the country and annually sponsor a dinner for high school scholar athletes in their area. They need to succeed. Otherwise, the leaders of intercollegiate sports, including ADs from all three divisions, are merely rearranging the deck chairs and maintaining the status quo.

Responsibility for the future of college athletics and the values it teaches lies squarely in the hands of university presidents, boards of trustees, ADs, conference officials, and the NCAA. They can challenge the system of corruption that has become the norm in the pursuit of money. Or they can take the easy path by betraying their responsibilities and claiming, "We can't do anything about it." Then they have failed the most important constituents—all of their student athletes.

RUTGERS AND SOME FINAL WORDS

Rutgers University's athletics program was set on a solid path between 1998 and 2008. I regret that leadership has since strayed off course, and there have been shameful incidents involving student athletes' and coaches' actions off the field.

Those challenges are not unique to Rutgers; they confront intercollegiate sports programs and athletic leadership across higher education in America.

I am encouraged by the new direction Rutgers athletics chose early in 2016. The school now has proven leadership committed to resetting the proper coordinates for Big Ten athletic strategy overall and football specifically.

Situations I dealt with as a young naval officer remind me of the issues confronting Division I college sports today. On January 17, 1961, I was serving as a reserve officer in the U.S. Navy. It was three days before John F. Kennedy would be sworn into office as the 35th president of the United States.

That evening, President Eisenhower, in his farewell address to the nation, made a historic reference to the growth of military power in the world: "We recognize the imperative need for this development. Yet we must not fail to comprehend its grave implications. In the councils of government, we must guard against the acquisition of unwarranted influence, whether sought or unsought, by the military industrial complex. The potential for the disastrous rise of misplaced power exists and will persist."[8]

President Eisenhower could have been speaking about today's intercollegiate industrial complex. Some of his warnings about misplaced power and unwarranted influence could apply to NCAA Division I programs.

Normally, public scandals create a constituency that demands change. From politicians being voted out or forced to resign to corporate boards removing CEOs, there is often definitive action driven by public outcry that simultaneously costs jobs and leads to reform.

In college athletics, most of the outrage concerning scandals tends to be centered in the media. Can those advocating true reform in college athletics motivate a public and create a constituency to truly drive change? Yes, a coach or AD may lose his or her job, but that Power Five school's fan base wants a winner.

So this question is complicated by the political reality that in any number of southern and midwestern states, a legendary football or basketball coach may have more power than the college president or even the governor (i.e., Alabama or North Carolina). Do those coaches' partisan constituencies care more about reform or winning?

The only realistic solution—because I don't see the NCAA being capable in its current form—is to return authority to the conferences and hope that strong leadership will right the ship. This would likely require either creating a new oversight body or reforming how the NCAA now operates. The alternatives don't offer much hope because of various external forces, as I have explained. It's time to clearly define the mission and then follow it. Is the leadership committed to accomplishing what needs to be done? I am concerned.

Good leaders clearly define a mission because they know where they are going. They communicate how to accomplish this—together, as one team. They constantly inspire and praise good work. They set an example by sharing success and credit with everyone who takes them to the goal line.

These were bedrock traits and values we followed in my decade at Rutgers, but more importantly, they've been my guiding principles throughout my professional career and the approach Terry and I took with raising our seven children. I may not have always been successful, but I certainly have strived to practice them each day of my life.

LET US BEGIN

ACKNOWLEDGMENTS

My grateful and heartfelt thanks go first to Robert Stewart—a gentleman, an author of several acclaimed books, and Rutgers University graduate—for his work with me on this labor of love from the very beginning of the process.

To John Samerjan, John Wooding, and Marian Rosenwasser, longtime associates who spent countless hours working with me on this project and contributed significantly, my sincere thanks.

My daughter Deidre, RU '03, who spent many hours helping put this project together and see it through to completion—I love you and have so enjoyed working with you.

Thank you to my Villanova roommate and lifelong friend Jack Kelly, who was so generous and encouraging in making this book become a reality.

To my entire staff, coaches, associates, and all of the behind-the-scenes staff, including facilities and maintenance at Rutgers University who made it happen day in and day out, we worked together as a family to bring the success we had in that decade from 1998 to 2008. I appreciate all of your hard work and commitment to our collective successes.

And finally, to all of the donors who so generously contributed to us from the earliest days and have become lifelong friends, notably Jon Hanson and Finn Wentworth—I am truly grateful.

NOTES

FOREWORD

1. Editorial, *Observer Tribune*, April 4, 1974.

2. John F. Kennedy, "Annual Message to the Congress on the State of the Union," speech delivered before a joint session, January 14, 1963, American Presidency Project, https://www.presidency.ucsb.edu/documents/annual-message-the-congress-the -state-the-union-3.

3. "Address at the National Football Foundation and Hall of Fame Banquet, 5 December 1961," John F. Kennedy Presidential Library and Museum Archives, https://www.jfklibrary.org/asset-viewer/archives/JFKWHA/1961/JFKWHA-060 -002/JFKWHA-060-002.

4. Brendan Byrne, "How Do You Feel about Rutgers Firing Bob Mulcahy?," *Newark Star Ledger*, December 22, 2008.

5. Herb Jaffe, "Mulcahy Legend Grows Steadily without Fanfare," *Newark Star Ledger*, December 14, 1993.

6. Richard Sandomir, "Strong Sports Agency Key in Yankee Saga," *New York Times*, October 25, 1993, https://www.nytimes.com/1993/10/25/nyregion/strong -sports-agency-key-in-yankee-saga.html.

7. Jerry Izenberg, "The Man Who Brought Home the Longshot," *Newark Star Ledger*, March 10, 1996.

CHAPTER 1 — WHY RUTGERS?

1. Vaughn McKoy, *Playing Up* (New Brunswick, N.J.: McKoy Group, 2013).

CHAPTER 4 — REBUILDING A PROGRAM

1. Comments from President McCormick to the cabinet during the state budget crisis of 2006.

2. Terry Beachem, "Shift in Financial Process," email to the author, 2017.

3. Beachem.

4. "The 1000 Men and Women of Rutgers," Rutgers 1000, n.d., http://www.ru1000 .org/RU1000.html.

5. "Student Right-to-Know Act," Cameron University, n.d., http://www.cameron .edu/iraa/srtk.

CHAPTER 5 — THE DON IMUS INCIDENT

1. Ryan Chiachiere, "Imus Called Women's Basketball Team 'Nappy-Headed Hos,'" *Media Matters for America*, April 4, 2007, https://www.mediamatters.org/ research/2007/04/04/imus-called-womens-basketball-team-nappy-headed/ 138497.

2. Associated Press, "Rutgers Women's Team, Coach Speak Out," *ESPN*, April 11, 2007, http://www.espn.com/ncw/news/story?id=2831636.

CHAPTER 6 — UPHOLDING TRADITIONS

1. Jerry Izenberg, "RU Became Tranghese's Ace in the Hole," *Newark Star Ledger*, November 9, 2006.

CHAPTER 9 — PROUD, WITH NO REGRETS

1. Athletic Review Committee (ARC) Report, Rutgers University, November 18, 2008, 10.

2. Jerry Izenberg, "Rutgers, an Amazing Season," *Newark Star Ledger*, 2007, 5.

3. Bob Braun, "Rutgers Football Is Bigger Than Rutgers," *Newark Star Ledger*, December 22, 2008, http://arolla.rssing.com/browser.php?indx=2087732&last=1& item=4.

CHAPTER 10 — AFTER RUTGERS, AND LEADING ISSUES

FOR NCAA SPORTS

1. Graham Couch, "Couch: Rutgers Climbed to Big Ten against Long Odds," *Lansing State Journal*, November 21, 2014, https://www.lansingstatejournal.com/story/sports/columnists/graham-couch/2014/11/21/couch-column-rutgers-big-ten/19353201/.

2. "About the Knight Commission," Knight Commission, n.d., https://www.knightcommission.org/#home-hero-tab-0.

3. "Keeping Faith with the Student-Athlete," Knight Commission, March 1991, 14–46, https://www.knightcommission.org/wp-content/uploads/2008/10/1991-93_kcia_report.pdf.

4. "'A Solid Start': A Report on Reform of Intercollegiate Athletics," Knight Commission, March 1992, 47–58, https://www.knightcommission.org/wp-content/uploads/2008/10/1991-93_kcia_report.pdf.

5. "A New Beginning for a New Century: Intercollegiate Athletics in the United States," Knight Commission, March 1993, 59–70, https://www.knightcommission.org/wp-content/uploads/2008/10/1991-93_kcia_report.pdf.

6. Juliet Macur, "N.C.A.A.'s Vote on New Rules Creating Divisions among Conferences," *New York Times*, August 7, 2014, https://www.nytimes.com/2014/08/08/sports/ncaas-vote-on-new-rules-contradicts-its-mission.html.

7. Marc Tracy, "N.C.A.A. Votes to Give Richest Conferences More Autonomy," *New York Times*, August 7, 2014, https://www.nytimes.com/2014/08/08/sports/ncaafootball/ncaa-votes-to-give-greater-autonomy-to-richest-conferences.html.

8. Maria Dinzeo, "Federal Judge Overturns NCAA Restrictions on Athletes Income," Court House News, August 8, 2014, https://www.courthousenews.com/federal-judge-overturns-ncaarestrictions-on-athletes-income/.

9. Steve Berkowitz, "Judge Releases Ruling on O'Bannon Case: NCAA Loses," *USA Today*, August 8, 2014, https://www.usatoday.com/story/sports/college/2014/08/08/ed-obannon-antitrust-lawsuit-vs-ncaa/13801277/.

10. Joe Palazzo, "A Quarterback's Lawsuit over Videogame Renews Danger to N.C.A.A.," *Wall Street Journal*, May 21, 2013, https://www.wsj.com/articles/SB10001424127887323648304578497849470449718436.

11. Ryan Hart v. Electronic Arts, Inc., No. 11-3750 (3d Cir. 2012), https://www.eff.org/files/hart_v._ea_3rd_cir_decision_copy.pdf.

12. Ryan Hart v. Electronic Arts.

13. Joe Nocera, "Opinion: She Had to Tell What She Knew," *New York Times*, May 5, 2014, https://www.nytimes.com/2014/05/06/opinion/nocera-she-had-to-tell -what-she-knew.html.

14. Mike Krzyzewski, *The Gold Standard* (New York: Grand Central, 2009).

15. Tom Farley, "Study: 1 in 27 Head Injuries Reported," *ABC News*, October 2, 2014, https://abcnews.go.com/Sports/study-27-head-injuries-reported/story?id=25932616.

16. "Did NCAA Ignore Concussion Issue?," Fox Sports, November 4, 2013, https:// www.foxsports.com/collegefootball/story/ncaa-concussion-lawsuit-mediation -harder-time-than-nfl-defending-itself-110413.

17. Sarah Ganim, "Unnecessary Roughness? Players Question NCAA's Record on Concussions," CNN, http://www.cnn.com/interactive/2014/10/us/ncaa-concussions/ index.html.

18. Ganim.

19. "Tommy John Surgeries Increasing for Youth Athletes," American Ortho- paedic Society for Sports Medicine, July 12, 2015, https://www.sciencedaily.com/ releases/2015/07/150712203819.htm.

20. Jim Delany, "Education First, Athletics Second: The Time for a National Dis- cussion Is upon Us," April 17, 2015, http://files.ctctcdn.com/c7876417001/2bfcbc02 -7b5f-4ff5-9229-4f2a0f2d620e.pdf.

21. Delany.

22. Delany.

23. Delany.

24. Delany.

25. Delany.

26. Delany.

27. "Position Statement: Freshman Ineligibility in Intercollegiate Athletics," Drake Group, April 20, 2015, https://drakegroupblog.files.wordpress.com/2015/04/ tdg-freshman-ineligibility-position-paper.pdf.

28. Dan Wolken, "Examining the Big Ten's Statement on Education, Athletics," *USA Today*, April 17, 2015, https://www.usatoday.com/story/sports/college/2015/04/ 17/big-ten-jim-delany-education-athletic-memo/25933525/.

CHAPTER 11 — A CALL FOR VALUES AND FINAL THOUGHTS

1. Howard J. Savage, *American College Athletics*, bulletin 23 (New York: Carnegie Foundation for the Advancement of Teaching, 1929), http://archive.carnegie foundation.org/pdfs/elibrary/American_College_Athletics.pdf.

2. Charles Clotfelter, "Big-Time College Athletics 80 Years Later," *Opinion, Athletics, Academics*, October 27, 2009, https://today.duke.edu/2009/10/clotfelter_oped .html.

3. Sharmeen Obaid-Chinoy and Trish Dalton, dir., *Student Life*, presented in association with LeBron James, Maverick Carter, and Jamal Henderson at Spring-Hill Entertainment and Steve Stoute at United Masters, HBO, October 2, 2018.

4. Keith Sergeant, "Which Big Ten Football Program Makes the Most Money? Who Spends the Most? Look at BiG Financials," NJ.com, April 5, 2018, https://www .nj.com/rutgersfootball/index.ssf/2018/04/look_at_what_each_big_ten_football _program_earned.html.

5. Keith Sergeant, "How Much Does Rutgers Spend on Men's Basketball and How It Compares in Big Ten?," NJ.com, April 5, 2018, https://www.nj.com/ rutgersbasketball/index.ssf/2018/04/how_much_does_rutgers_spend_on_mens _basketball_and.html.

6. "Position Statement: Freshman Ineligibility in Intercollegiate Athletics," Drake Group, April 20, 2015, https://drakegroupblog.files.wordpress.com/2015/04/tdg -freshman-ineligibility-position-paper.pdf.

7. Ken Reed, *How We Can Save Sports: A Game Plan* (Lanham, Md.: Rowman & Littlefield, 2015).

8. Dwight D. Eisenhower, "Farewell Address to the Nation," January 17, 1961, http://mcadams.posc.mu.edu/ike.htm.

INDEX

ABOUT THE AUTHOR

BOB MULCAHY has spent his entire career in service—since his days in the navy following his graduation from Villanova University to his time as chief of staff to former New Jersey governor Brendan Byrne, president and CEO of the Meadowlands, and athletic director at Rutgers University. His love and pride for New Jersey has always been evident and was one of the biggest motivations behind his decision to accept the position at Rutgers and bring the football program to the national stage.

Bob has played a primary role in many great moments in New Jersey history, including saving the Pinelands; hosting the World Cup, the NCAA Men's Basketball Final Four, and Pope John Paul II's visit to Giants Stadium; and bringing the New York Jets and the New Jersey Devils to the state.

His firsthand accounts of experiences in leadership are poignant reminders of what it means to have character and a moral compass.

Bob has served on several nonprofit boards, including 13 years as the chairman of Cathedral Healthcare in Newark, New Jersey; 14 years on the Atlantic Healthcare System board; and 21 years on the board of the National Football Foundation and College Hall of Fame. He has also served as the chairman of Georgian Court University Board of Trustees and as a charter trustee of the County College of Morris.

Bob and his wife, Terry, raised their family in Mendham, New Jersey, where they lived for 37 years before moving to Basking Ridge. They are the parents of seven children and numerous grandchildren.